R U B B L E

M A S O N R Y

RUBBLE
MASONRY

ROSE
McLARNEY

LOUISIANA STATE UNIVERSITY PRESS
BATON ROUGE

Published by Louisiana State University Press
lsupress.org

LSU Press Paperback Original

DESIGNER: Michelle A. Neustrom
TYPEFACES: Whitman, text; Gotham, display

COVER ILLUSTRATION: *On One Hand the Other*, 2016, by David Trautrimas.
Courtesy of the artist.

LIBRARY OF CONGRESS CATALOGING-IN-PUBLICATION DATA
Names: McLarney, Rose, 1982– author
Title: Rubble masonry / Rose McLarney.
Description: Baton Rouge : Louisiana State University Press, 2026.
Identifiers: LCCN 2025045776 (print) | LCCN 2025045777 (ebook) |
   ISBN 978-0-8071-8589-6 (paperback) | ISBN 978-0-8071-8627-5 (epub) |
   ISBN 978-0-8071-8628-2 (pdf)
Subjects: LCGFT: Essays
Classification: LCC PS3613.C5725 R83 2026 (print) | LCC PS3613.C5725 (ebook) |
   DDC 814/.6—dc23/eng/20251120
LC record available at https://lccn.loc.gov/2025045776
LC ebook record available at https://lccn.loc.gov/2025045777

to Suzette *and those who conceive of such hopes with me*

CONTENTS

▲

▲

AUTHOR'S NOTE

In these essays, I have made my best attempt to gather and present accurate historical, biological, and other information—as I understand it. However, names, identifying characteristics, and details of personal experiences have been changed. I have made these edits as a creative writer trying to most considerately and effectively tell stories that are true—as I remember them.

RUBBLE MASONRY

INSTRUCTIONS FOR CONDUCTING
A CEMETERY SURVEY

Study the tombstones and *make no changes or assumptions regarding missing or seemingly erroneous text*, says the guide for historical society volunteers.

So I record only *1876–1___* and do not guess what the latter figures are. Record only *Ponder* and do not venture to make the blurrier shapes into a first name.

Do not assume because two people are in the same plot that they are married or otherwise related. Report that they share the area but avoid making up what the relationship is, the guide further instructs.

I note *Breedlove, Breedlove,* and do not suppose wife, mother, daughter, or _____.

To discern worn letters, *Hold a mirror at ninety degrees to the side of the stone. The obliquely angled light should make the engravings' shadows clearer.*

I've come alone. Still, I carry a makeup compact, always. And think of mistakes and questions: How do you spend your days, where will they end, will there be a shared lot, partner in what, buried by and bearer of whom? And turn the mirror to my own face.

WEIGHTS AND MEASURES

The racehorse crossing the line shining clean because he never had to see another step in front of him, kicking back mud. The racehorse whom the viewers never for a moment had to consider in a position that wasn't first. That's how my grandfather thought of himself. *I always came out ahead*, he said.

My grandfather, who we are burying. In one-hundred-degree heat, the flowers sagging, sweat stains swagging the underarms of every shirt, logging trucks thundering by on the highway, waving their scrappy flags, not of triumph, on oversized loads of felled trees.

He would not have been determined a victor in seconds, feet, or furlongs— by any measure others share. But he would have fixed his eyes on the proud parts of the day with the focus of the honor guard come to give the military salute, firing guns in unison, folding the flag from his casket crisply, with a ceremony of utter certainty. The confidence with which some move through the world (particularly men, white, of a certain generation) . . . I am uncomfortable in the most basic element of existence, my flesh that my dress bunches against. But he fought hard to stay in his skin, no matter how it wizened.

For some horses, who do have mud flung in their eyes, it is a mercy, in that it blinds them to their place, to the finish ahead. We lower his body into the red clay.

▲

I became interested in horse racing after the competition, which lasts only seconds, flashed past on a TV, and my grandfather's passing. (The single sport I know is running, and I'd been losing my ability to do that too.)

It was the absences that drew me, initially. Noticing all the jockeys in the Derby seemed to be Latinx, reading about this, then reading about the disappearance of African Americans from the sport. African Americans did more than equally well as white contenders, they excelled, winning more than half of the early Kentucky Derbies. Then came segregation and its tensions, captured in the 1905 *Washington Post* headline "Negro Rider on Wane, White Jockeys' Superior Intelligence Supersedes." There have been few Black jockeys against which to measure performance since.

Then reading about purging—what jockeys do to lighten the horses' loads. Racing's lore is full of laxatives, tapeworms, amphetamines. Or rather the jockeys are emptied, stomachs' contents going into heaving bowls tracks openly provide. They sweat out and spit up as much as a half-pound of saliva in a day, dehydrating themselves as close to weightlessness as man can achieve.

Today half or more of the jockeys in the Triple Crown are Latinx. Weight (not inclusivity) might explain this rise. The average Panamanian or Mexican man is three inches shorter than the average U.S. man. There is less of a Latinx to get in the way. The pay is little. All that's high is rate of injury.

Then my interest came back, as interests tend to do, to a subject in which I see myself: women. The average American woman is four or five inches shorter than the average American man. Women have lower bone density and body mass. And they're more practiced in self-imposed starvation, leaders in that field. Yet light as women may be, there have been only six female jockeys in the Triple Crown races in all of its history.

During most visits, my grandfather would fit in an appraising stare and the phrase *I'm glad you haven't gotten heavy like the rest.* I've worked at getting nearer gone. Not over a course's finish line, not cleared from the field, but running myself too thin to win.

▲

Small comments carry weight. And slender shoulders?

A woman starts going to the gym. A month into her discipline, the scale registers higher. She hates herself for her failure. (She has lost fat and gained muscle, its density.) This is not light subject matter.

There is a difference in mass and weight. Mass is the actual amount of matter in an object. Weight is the pull of gravity exerted upon it.

Psychologists today say we should not approach anorexia as a concern with mere appearances but as an issue of the serious—grave—minded, as intellectual, moral, in nature. The anorexic winnows her figure down not to invite the appetites of men but to create a greater space between herself and others (thigh that does not spread toward the one she's seated beside, bone startling enough to avert a gaze). Consider Descartes, Kant, all the philosophers dividing the mind from the flesh; God's great sacrifice of putting Christ in the form of a body; the mystics and saints fasting toward transcendence; lightness as our language's metaphor for thought and conscience right and pure.

When the fitness instructor shouts at the woman to raise her arms, which are lifting weights, again and again, to imagine being *swans, swans,* what comes to her mind instead is flight's impossibility. And *pack animal, pack animal* as a call.

▲

Lighten the load, I think when I remember the stories of my grandfather as a child, many evenings carrying his father, too drunk to walk, home. I think of wings, prayers for intervention, directed to where it would take him ninety more years to ascend.

And *Give him a greater weight* is the thought that comes of the story of the child's first time picking cotton, skinny and hungry. He was to be paid by the pound and, filling a sack marked 25, thought his pockets and belly would bulge soon too. But the sack was sized for flour, its density. (He would work a ten-hour day.)

The rest of the story is that when the boy bore his father, over his shoulder, home, the man wore every piece of clothing he owned at once, because he had begun the day intending to find work. The man dressed, wishing to seem strong, bulky. The child's cargo was airier than, to a passerby, it looked to be. Which is good, which is bad? What is the scale by which to differentiate desirable substance and weight?

▲

In Aristotle's chariot allegory, a man steers two horses in a circuit between the earth and heavens. The white and temperate horse works to carry him upward to glimpse the godly. But the one is yoked to another.

The dark and lumbering horse pulls back toward the corporeal world, strains to follow his desire. Fields are green with what he can graze there. Is it any wonder the charioteer loses his grasp on the reins? Even the scholars of Greek seem torn, or hungry. In translations of the allegory, they use the words *nourishment* and *filling* to describe visions of enlightenment.

When the elderly pass away, we give praise, say they are in a better place. When they were too ill to eat, we had feeding tubes forced down their throats, cheered for every ounce of fat maintained, for every day they struggled and remained.

▲

No one in my family has ever owned a horse—a beast to be a burden to, a creature to lead and care for. Yet since the death of one of us, I've been strangely devoted to thinking of the taxonomic family Equidae. After all, not-knowing, omissions, are very much a part of fond feeling.

We hold the hardest secrets within ourselves if we can and use our own bodies to block view of disturbing scenes from loved ones. To continue being able to love those we do, we overlook bodies aging ugly, character flaws we call *human*. And those who are masters of horses blinder them— the enormity of their eyes, the largest of any land mammal.

It is not too limiting to reduce horses' capacity to take in everything within 360 degrees, riders will claim. A horse is, by nature, a spook-prone animal of prey, watchful even when its head is down in the hay. Blinders make this life pleasanter. Or, it could be said, they let the wearer keep moving on and beyond this troubling place, through whatever race must be run to the pasture waiting at the end.

The Irish had a custom of putting horse skulls beneath their floors. The horse's head is of such great volume that when dead and emptied, the remaining vessel of bone creates an echo. (Spatial volume become aural. Space, if not with the physical, filled.) People wanted to live in a house with this sound, they wanted to walk—and dance—over the percussive floor. Proudly, they would stuff into the eye socket a piece of paper inscribed with the family name. The rest they would leave to gape. Let the absence resonate.

BLUEPRINTS

—for my maternal grandmother, Elizabeth Ervin, née Barringer

I saw the blueprint
of your apartment.
Edna always
shows me the letters,
Mama also.
Seems we should be
talking color schemes,
picking cotton,
and hunting apples
in the leaves. (Ha)
They are all gone
now you know.

Reading the lines tailored to a slender slip of paper, I read into the breaks. A break bares the bleakness in the parentheses, twisting the *Ha* bitterly, like a dejected speaker's lip. A break pauses after *They are all gone* so the reader can think back from the leaves to the people who would go too. A break makes *now you know* a heavier declaration by standing it alone.

This is the first among the letters to my grandmother, Elizabeth (as I must get used to her being addressed). Elizabeth, age seventeen, had just married and moved from the family farm in North Carolina to where her husband would work in Washington, DC. The writer is an aunt I never met. She is near Elizabeth's age and, at the time, also recently married.

In North Carolina, the unmarried women of a household had all slept in a single bed. In DC, the bed is only something the family can inquire about as a movable object, wondering how, among other furniture, it has been positioned.

▲

A note Elizabeth's much younger sister adds is a study in contrast to the aunt's, in that it leaves no space.

> *roses are blooming very pretty and pink I am going to send you a rose a bud*
> *so it will last a long time and you can put it in water and it will last a long*
> *time and you can watch it bloom that little bud will be me 8 more days and*
> *my school year ends love nelly*

Stanza, as many poets know, is the Italian word for *room*, and in this letter without any such divisions, the girl is herself unfolding into Elizabeth's home—they are sharing quarters again. The sentences run on, right over the implications of aging and change, making their case for continuation, straight to Nelly's name.

▲

Nelly does not crowd out the aunt, but rather helps me see her more clearly. How she is expert in pause, repeatedly drawn away from the letters to tend pots or babies, her return marked by changes between pencil and pen. And constantly reconsidering the value of their small country news, and what she can do.

> *My hand wobbles like a new calf. By the way, we have a new calf. Oh, but I'm*
> *not practiced at this. There's so much that needs erasing.*

An expert on language might be able to explain away some of the lack of confidence here, help dwell on the courtesy of her phrases. *Exchanging floors* is linguists' term for the way women interrupt their own speech, when they are able to converse in person, with *um, sort of, but, a bit, it seems, who am I to say,* providing places for a listener to enter.

▲

Another letter, after more seasons passed, asks,

> *Did you know the cherries are ripe here?*
> *That the baby has little shoes?*
> *But the bottoms are soft.*

It is tempting to be jealous of the letter writers who may presume distances can be spanned, answers to their inquiries will come. They can do this because they are not yet addressing the dead.

The half of a correspondence left in the dark of the deceased's house are replies—not necessarily in the voice of the one who was dear to the inheritor. I want the words of my grandmother, long gone to the grave. What I get are a small box of strangers' questions and the gaping blanks following them.

▲

The questions the aunt asks are of the politest kind. And the amendment, after telling about the baby's shoes—*But the bottoms are soft*—is meant to soften the blow. To ease Elizabeth's realization of time elapsing and what she no longer knows. (At least the baby has not grown so that he can stand tall, walk out of the frame of reference, the mind's gilt-edged image of home.)

Comfort, not foreboding, is what that first narrow letter was intended to convey. The writer was making use of scraps. The family was poor. But for a while, they were fortunate that when letters stopped, it only meant they had run out of paper, not that there had been a greater loss.

When the crops had been harvested or there was work at the mill, the aunt's letters are on stationery and full of the digits of yardages for curtains she'll make and cents spent on setting up her own home.

> *They bought me two of the prettiest gowns you ever saw. They are real silk ($6.95), baby blue.*

Details, but not all the story. I have to put together from others' letters that she could not go to town to do her own shopping, was bedridden in the finery.

No mention of the death of her brother in a plane crash, the war he was training for. Such facts must be gathered from clipped bits of newspaper.

While she writes, *There's a dress I'm going to sew.*

Then as a favorable description, *The fabric is soldier blue.*

And there's this:

> *Having a husband and housekeeping are hard. You and I never suffered so much working in the fields, really. But he is going to tint the ceilings sky blue.*

It is only after I have become curious and press those who have survived her that I learn what she couldn't put in writing. The truth about her husband. About the color of bruising, the eye blackening, her bones—

In the letters, she is trying to give what the lonely recipient wants to hear, girlish memories of working outside, not under the roof or given into the hands of anybody.

▲

Closing our letters with our own names, we mean to make a gesture of generosity. Mean please reply, send signs you're there, an envelope to unseal like peeling petals from a flower (even if the outside has shriveled and dried), seeking the color it was alive.

So, I have letters from my great-grandaunt. (Is that the correct combination of words with which to designate her? Should *removed* be in there?) She was a woman who died before I was born, at age forty-five. I fill in as best I can, and this reading has given me some company, somewhere to stand (on the scrubbed linoleum floor of an old kitchen of my envisioning).

Throughout the woman's funeral, I've heard, the preacher called her by the wrong name. Nobody stopped him. But her words are here still, what I write of today comes from pages signed *Lucille*.

I'll end, and not be done with that name, then. Build with what measures there are, based on what lines have been given. Imagine being among young women, running out into wide fields. No one bound, nothing broken, convincing each other the blue of our lives should be the color of *sky*.

STORIED

—after *Homeplace: The Social Use and Meaning of the Folk Dwelling in Southwestern North Carolina,* by Michael Ann Williams

I-houses are houses that are only one room deep—and two stories high.

Once, when I was a child in the mountains of what we now call western North Carolina, an I-house is what I thought I wanted to grow up and own. They were tall and slender, seemed high reaching yet austere.

I-houses, when they appeared in the region in the 1840s and 1850s, marked an architectural departure from the single-story cabins that preceded them. In addition to their second level, I've read, I-houses had the distinctive interior feature of an entry hall.

Upstairs, residents' perhaps-strewn blankets or possible states of undress were kept at a discreet remove from those who might drop by. The hall blocked viewing too. A visitor had to wait, after gaining access through the front door, to be asked to come farther. Meanwhile, dishes and other messes could be tidied away.

I didn't know any of this as a girl, though. I hadn't been invited into such a home, hadn't gotten far enough to encounter a hall yet. I began desiring I-houses from the outside, looking toward roof and sky.

The statements their historic shapes made must have appealed to me because my family had moved to the county after my birth. Unlike the truly local kids, I did not have a name carried on from the early white settlers, shared by schools and roads.

The B. family's house is an I-house a few miles' distance from and more than a century older than my family's house (a construction completed when I had already begun talking). I saw the B. house from the back seat of my parents' car as they drove out where pastures were overgrown and we could trespass and pick blackberries in summer, cut cedars for Christmas trees. Saw it as I tried to prepare for my driver's license test on back roads, my father as passenger, covering his eyes. During college breaks when I could come home, I would slow down for the sight sometimes as I ran by, having turned a visitor to the county.

I moved farther away, pursued a career in poetry, and took Southern Appalachia and its culture as subject matter. Yet it would be years until I investigated I-houses and their origins, thought beyond their facades.

I thought myself unstoried—that was my virtue—as a young writer. I tried to use words to capture bowhunters who dreamed of bear, devoted pages to the husbandmen of cattle. Thought other figures' significance and their narratives, like the mountains, towered over my own autobiography. And what critics of the time liked was for women poets to *get the I out.*

Lately, I've been returning to that hardscrabble pastoral by reading in the fields of history and architecture. I've been studying western North Carolina. I can acquire, if not acreage, information, at least.

From Michael Ann Williams's book *Homeplace: The Social Use and Meaning of the Folk Dwelling in Southwestern North Carolina,* I learn that the standard I-house concept has a ground level with a center hall, a front door entering it, and a room opening from either side.

The B. house's floor plan varies from this. Instead, I have heard, it is a row of three individual rooms, each accessible only by its own exterior door.

Even I-houses that had initially adhered to convention were modified after they were occupied for a while. Residents discovered the spaces in the entries felt wasted and set up sewing machines and beds in the halls. And I-houses got passed on over time. Inheritors thought the barriers were uncomfortable and undertook renovations, tearing down walls.

This was just the beginning of the outdating and updating (the wood floors covered with linoleum, then with carpet, and so on) that the houses document.

There never is just one version of a thing. What's old is layered and testament to change.

But when you hear arguments for exceptions and for not being concerned by how things were, you can guess there was trouble with the usual preceding state. You might wonder what someone present needs redemption from.

The caller left unattended long enough in a house's foyer gets curious about the reality of how the house is run, peeks behind and into this and that.

The chorus of a Greek tragedy, poet Dan Beachy-Quick writes in "The 'I' of Lyric," *stood aside from the narrated event, from those speakers of action, seeking some fact it knew must exist, but of which it could feel only the vestige, only its troubled absence.*

Here's more history I've learned: The appearance of I-houses in western North Carolina in the 1840s and 1850s coincided with the expansion of slavery into the region. Slavery had been legal in what would become the United States for over two hundred years before railroads extended into the remote Appalachian Mountains, introducing among the subsistence farmers profiteers of the plantation economy. And while I-houses concealed some elements of their tenants' daily routines, they revealed larger truths. They were discriminating.

Most poets I've known don't want their work to be perceived as confessional—as baring the self, oversharing in some weepy, too-fleshy way. In an interview, poet Lisa Lewis (speaking, strategically, in the second person) says that the label *confessional* can be like a *wasp in the room: you hope it stays near the ceiling where it can't hurt anybody.*

At the time of the Civil War, people in older, lower cabins (with ceilings that would touch a contemporary person's head), staying closer to the dirt they hoed, might be assumed pro-Union, some of their descendants today like to say. The owners of the loftier I-houses were more likely to be enslavers and support the Confederacy.

When I found that the name *I-house* derives from the states of Indiana, Iowa, and Illinois, I was just strangely glad for my own sake. Of what I'd once wanted to be mine, I then wished to say: Let them have those old white structures.

The B. house was once a display of wealth larger than the family could have earned with their own labor, without enslaving people.

White as I am, may I be pleased to come from a family without title to much real estate (or chattel), of drifters too poor for record to have been made of their power?

I am no relation to the B. family.

Still, I've been told about them and their home. I know the doors are all an external show. There are no internal doors on the first floor. So, to get from the bedroom to the kitchen meant going out one front door, across the porch, into another door. I know the first little girl to live there was carried by her parents between rooms, wrapped in a blanket, when it was cold.

The tradition of the chorus did not end with ancient Greeks. The lyric *I* in contemporary poetry speaks as an individual while providing a portal to collective experiences greater than just hers.

My mother knows a woman who knows the woman whose mother was a child when the B. house was new. She was a friend of the girl who lived there. So the particulars, the human interest and touching details of the story, have been shared with me. Under the cover of patchwork and a dusting of snow, I know, despite it being so many years ago, that *Frances* was the B. girl's given name.

While the chorus may have led the action, they followed along with the narrative, they too arrived at its heartbreaking end. The actor who cedes the lead is not relieved of playing the remaining undesirable roles.

If the eye is to observe, however outward the gaze is directed, it must be in a body that is part of the scene. In her essay "The Little Death of Self," Marianne Boruch reminds us about poems, *Someone writes these things.* And, *Who wants with such passion to do in that "I"? I do I do I do* . . .

There is no letting the *I* get away. So here I am, back in my home county, at the B. house again. As I stand in the public road, staring at the building, a storm blows over the Cowee Mountains and across the Little Tennessee River. If my ancestors' shelters were too small and humble to last, the fact that the land was named by the Cherokee Nation remains. *Cowee, Tennessee*—they are not in a language I can speak or that belongs to anybody in my line. So what can I come closer to calling mine, what must I claim?

The B. house has been abandoned, and the heirs aren't the kind with money for repairs. A former *No Trespassing* sign, with all but the barest hints of the letters worn away, waves, catches my eye. Three rusty doorknobs hang from their three holes, a welcome, repeated and underscored (didn't you wish for this this this?). But I know now they're no shelter, these places open for me to step into.

Coda

In closing, or to continue with what's beyond the house, I turn the page over to Allison Adelle Hedge Coke, a poet who was raised partly in North Carolina and identifies as of Native descent. This is an excerpt—with a refrain of *I* that speaks for a generous *we*—from her "America, I Sing You Back." The poem is dedicated to the poet's own father, Robert Hedge Coke, in addition to Phil Young, Walt Whitman, and Langston Hughes.

> But here I am, here I am, here I remain high on each and every peak, carefully rumbling her great underbelly, prepared to pour forth singing—
>
> and sing again I will, as I have always done.
>
> Never silenced unless in the company of strangers, singing
>
> the stoic face, polite repose, polite while dancing deep inside, polite Mother of her world. Sister of myself.

DEVELOPMENT OPPORTUNITY

Waiting in line to board the bus as a fourth grader, I overheard a third grader say he'd never date a girl who didn't shave. I had never noticed him before; school kids don't notice those the level below. He was scrawny, and I wasn't even sure of his name—Darrell? Still he had reason to dismiss me—

As soon as I got home, I went to the bathroom, found a razor, and began with my shin. I went at the effort with vigor and pressure; I did not know about the role of soap and water. The blood stained my shorts, it coursed to the floor. It was more than I could conceal from my mother. And so she had to teach me how to shave, though she hadn't wanted me to have such concerns about appearances yet.

My family's house faces the river, and across it, the valley rises into a mountain. For years, sitting on our porch, with a view of the mountainside, I imagined owning the land, in possession of enough understanding to know it would need preservation. But today I must admit I was never the kind of woman who will earn much or marry into money. A banner has gone up announcing the property for sale. I can read it from the porch swing. The price of two million dollars. Beside *Call me* and the picture of the realtor—Darrell.

Now is the most I can wish that my mother will not be alive, or sharp enough, to see the subdividers' bulldozers gash through the brush, into the red clay?

CIRCLING

It was a plaza of discount stores, where, in second grade, my mother bought sneakers with Velcro closures for me so the other kids would not notice I had not learned to tie my shoes. Location of the gas station bathroom, where, as sophomores, cross-country team members would hide during practice, smoking cigarettes, secrets that made us feel older and that we bonded over keeping from the adults.

Now it's the site where the town's greenway is being expanded and a sculpture will be placed. The sculpture will depict a Cherokee woman offering corn to an enslaved woman who shares the handle of a basket with the daughter of settlers. These are historical figures from my home county in North Carolina. The sculpture's title is *Sowing the Seeds of the Future*.

It is rare that women are monumentalized. But I have learned of some examples from the book *Monuments to the Lost Cause*, edited by Cynthia Mills and Pamela H. Simpson. There is a statue of a Confederate memorial in Raleigh, North Carolina, dedicated in 1914, of a woman and child seated together. The child has his hand on a sword; she is holding a book. It's not exclusively a woman who is represented—the boy is there in the space too, to make her a mother figure—but she features large.

It is *bullshit*, says a detractor of *Sowing the Seeds of the Future*. Three such women would have never held hands.

In the 1920s, a North Carolina senator had proposed a monument *in memory of the faithful slave mammies of the South*—a woman holding a white baby, with Black toddlers' hands tugging at her skirt.

Sowing the Seeds of the Future is not meant to suggest that such individuals danced in a literal circle with each other, says the project leader. It is to show that they lived in the same time, same region.

The boy in the Raleigh statue has been interpreted as offering the possibility of either taking the blade from the scabbard or having just returned it, evoking both the past of his forefathers and looking ahead to the future. The Confederate woman is believed to be educating the boy about the Lost Cause and southern culture. They both appear to be white.

The hometown sculpture project leader, the detractor, and I are all white.

The Raleigh Confederate woman's book pages are blank.

Information on the white settler appearing in *Sowing the Seeds of the Future*, Timoxena, is available because her descendants had a box of her papers, which they passed along to the town newspaper editor, who came up with the sculpture idea. When she, a widow, developed cancer, a friend and collaborator on *Sowing the Seeds of the Future* cared for her. And when the editor died, that caretaker carried on as the leader of the sculpture project.

In Confederate sculptures of females, they usually represent all white southern women in a general way, as embodiments of both the glory and the tragedy of the South. Historically, most sculptures with feminine figures, regardless of the occasion or country, have not been of a particular individual but, rather, symbols of abstract virtues such as justice or victory.

Of the Cherokee woman in the proposed statue, Rebecca, there are some records. Though she changed her first name from Na-Ka and married a white man, she had not surrendered enough to accept that it was his name that should appear on documents such as the title to her land.

The mammy statue proposed by the senator had a heavy, coarse shape. She was implicitly supposed to reassure the viewer that no history of exploiting Black bodies for not just labor but pleasure had occurred. Supposed to show Black women as having no sexual appeal to white men. Or to put it another way, she was to enshrine the myth of white women as comparably delicate and desirable.

If there were female figures held up for me by my community when I was young, I suppose they were collectible Barbies still sealed in the boxes with cellophane windows, displayed on shelves in friends' houses.

In the early 1900s, the United Daughters of the Confederacy declined to approve a female statue proposal because, as one member wrote, the woman portrayed in it didn't look how some thought their foremothers ought to but, rather, like a *willowy, sentimental, frivolous girl.* Were they defending realistic standards for the appearance of their gender? Or was this a case of women turning on other women, as we can do, afraid of the threat of another's greater beauty?

The papers included a photo of Timoxena in wedding attire, from which the sculptor sketched an accurate portrayal, detailing lace textures to etch in metal. The sculpture committee did not approve of the first draft of Timoxena's figure styled this way. They sent the sculptor back to draw her again in a plain dress and boots because the editor had left notes indicating she was the *workingest lady around.*

When I was a child, my mother took me out to the gardens where she worked. Ever resourceful, if a cucumber somehow managed to escape her notice and grew too big to eat, she'd turn it into a toy for me. She'd cut off one end, hollow the seeds out, carve an open-mouthed face, wrap a scrap of fabric around the bottom, and give me a spoon to feed it mud. This was a cucumber doll that dirtied its diaper. I'd change and care for the cucumber, watching my mother till and hoe, admiring her. (A baby doll is not the figure on which girls model themselves, of course; it is what is given to them so they can practice acting like conventional grown women.)

The newspaper editor was the first woman to ever serve in the position in my hometown. And, in the insular rural community where she had no kin, she was considered a newcomer, ever since moving from Atlanta to western North Carolina in the 1970s. She must have been honored to be entrusted with the legacy of Timoxena. The newspaper editor must have wanted Timoxena to be revered. How journalistically objective could she be about the slaveholder?

My mother's efforts, great as they were, could not change our whole culture. She sewed a soft doll with a child's shape out of pale-peach fabric she ordered just for this project for me, named her Iris. When I got home from a friend's house, I bound Iris's pliable middle tight with ribbon to give her a waist and try to push up a bust. I said I wanted a store-bought doll, like a normal girl.

What little is known of Salley, the enslaved woman in *Sowing the Seeds of the Future,* has been deduced from receipts. From the antebellum sale of her to Rebecca's husband, Salley's birth date was estimated. From the receipt showing her sale to Timoxena's husband, we can see the connection between them all. Both the Native and the settler family enslaved Salley.

The Daughters of the Confederacy raised substantial funds for memorials all over the South. In times when women had little power, they exercised this influence over money and public spaces. But of course, I cannot defend their project of constructing a false narrative, denying that the Civil War was fought for the sake of the institution of slavery.

My family does not have many roots in the county where I grew up. But we have a part in history, and I have a part in the story of *Sowing the Seeds of the Future* too. The person who opposes it for whitewashing was my high school civics teacher. The leader of the sculpture project is my uncle's wife—second wife, no blood relation.

These days, I teach at a university in Alabama, so there's more history that's mine to reckon with now. Alabama is home to several pieces of public art related to its famously racist heritage including the *National Monument for Peace and Justice,* monuments to civil rights marchers in Kelly Ingram Park in Birmingham, and *The Mothers of Gynecology* sculpture in

Montgomery. *The Mothers of Gynecology* is dedicated to Black women, in recognition of horrific experimentation they endured without anesthesia or consent, for the purpose of medical advancements from which others would benefit.

Where, in what period of history, could women really be represented as dancing together? Predecessors and outsiders and others hand in hand? The hometown sculpture project organizer, married into my family, who is not my cousin's mother or mother's sister—have we even brought her into our circle?

How much does anyone share, have in common or not, with anyone else living in proximity to them? It is an enormous question for some human-sized pieces of metal to raise.

Rebecca's house, located near the present sculpture site, was torched while her husband was away. When she ran from the flames, her acres were seized by men who justified their actions by saying the land was not occupied.

When I moved to Tulsa, Oklahoma, for a job and missed the North Carolina mountains, I would walk in the park across from my rental house. There, past the rose gardens, was the *Five Moons* sculpture, homage to the famous Native ballerinas Yvonne Chouteau, Rosella Hightower, Moscelyne Larkin, Maria Tallchief, and Marjorie Tallchief.

Eventually, Rebecca and her husband moved away from North Carolina to Indian Territory (now Oklahoma) because that's where more than seventy members of their family had been forcibly relocated or fled to.

The Cherokee traveled to Oklahoma on the Trail of Tears, and there is no way I could construe my choice to relocate for my career as similar to the ethnic cleansing by which they were driven from their ancestral lands. But in Tulsa, far from my family, I was comforted by the familiarity of place names (such as Coweta) derived from the Cherokee, similar to those in my mountains (Coweeta).

Rebecca didn't leave North Carolina without a fight. Her name appeared in print again before her departure. On a suit she filed that won her three thousand dollars (though not her property's return).

The Mothers of Gynecology seeks to restore to women whose bodies were sacrificed their personal identities, honoring, specifically, Anarcha, Lucy, and Betsey.

I haven't seen most of my schoolmates since I graduated. When I drive back to North Carolina, before I reach my parents' dirt road, I pass the greenway and women speed walking through the space where the statue will eventually stand. If I were a bit closer, going slower, I know I would know some of those faces as former girls'—now wrinkled and worn, weighted or under concealing foundation—instantly, still. And I wonder whether, if we met, I would be better or worse than whatever they'd imagined I'd become.

Often people who encountered the Native ballerina sculpture in the Tulsa park were inspired to pose in jokey, clumsy versions of their pirouettes, arabesques, piqués, jetés (or other positions, described by other terms I don't know enough about to appropriately apply). I was drawn to do the same but was too shy to reveal my gracelessness beside the statues' elegantly elongated bodies.

Local women modeled for *Sowing the Seeds of the Future.* Cherokee advisors asked that the sketch be revised again because, initially, the Cherokee woman was posed crouching, at lower level, lesser stature, than the rest.

Marjorie Tallchief's likeness was stolen, cut from *Five Moons* and removed from the park, a few years after I'd moved on from Tulsa for another job. Her absence becoming a monument to bigotry against Native people, women, art, beauty.

The speed walkers on the greenway create, with their pace, what seems to be an image of advancing forward. But that is rarely the quest of women's fitness. Many of us want to go back, or at least pause time, to look like we always have—or used to. Those who have changed the least since they were teenagers are both admired for it and hated a little bit.

To be honest, I've never cared for bronze sculptures in cities. I've never found realistic bronze renderings of commissioned sentiments innovative or complex like the art I'd choose, if I had funds and could make such decisions.

And maybe I associate public sculpture with the marble Confederate men standing in most every southern town square. If these monuments do anything better than cause fear and give a false sense of who is a hero and what's of value, they serve as reminders of parts of the past that it's tempting, more comfortable, to forget.

I took interest in bronze sculpture only when my mother told me about the process for the hometown statue. The bronze sculptor begins by making a maquette, a small model in clay. Next he makes a mold, impressions in relief. Lastly, a foundry casts the solid piece that will be displayed. Such replication and replication and expansion—

Most of the Marjorie Tallchief statue's pieces, after having been chopped apart, were recovered from various scrapyards. The sculptor is now recasting the missing bits and soldering her back together.

My knowledge of the adults that childhood friends have turned into is fragmental, gathered from a selfie on social media (posed at the ubiquitous angle) or an arrest record (that I judge to be expected). Or a flyer for a cancer fundraiser or an obituary I can barely believe is real. These send me back, wholly, into memory, where we inhabit our young, light bodies, and when we fall while playing tag or pursuing some ball, our skinned knees heal quickly.

Among the scraps of information pieced together to suppose a biography for Salley, there is this: a receipt for Timoxena paying Salley for a pound of spinning. The date is post–Civil War. It is basis for the guess that they relied on each other after Timoxena was widowed—and after Salley was emancipated.

The Mothers of Gynecology is made of materials gathered from scrapyards. These were the genesis, of the artist's process of creating the towering fifteen-foot figures. Donors contributed discards; the artwork is collective in that sense.

There are many layers to consider in thinking about the receipt for Salley's spinning. The receipt is from Timoxena's papers—she was the one with money to pay for another's labor. What the story continues to model, replicates post-slavery, are patterns of injustice. Yet also, it is said that Salley and Timoxena were lifelong friends, that they chose to stay together. And the caring those two humans seem to have shared should be passed on, made much of, too.

The pieces of stories I have collected are not equitable, their weights do not balance each other, they do not add up to a clear end.

But I pull my laces tight through the eyelets and set out to walk laps around the public path too.

SERVICE

Omar Khayyam, in the first millennium, in poems depicting God, the Creator, as a potter and people as his pots, wrote, *So many delicate heads, legs, hands, / Through whose love were they joined, by whose hatred smashed?*

The founder of Wedgwood pottery, in the 1700s, is said to have strode through his factories crushing the lesser products of his workers, shouting the assertion that they were *not good enough for Josiah Wedgwood.*

Wedgwood honed a process and a mixture of clay, ash, and bone to make china so fine that light could break through. He is remembered as a man who aspired to the highest quality.

Women still teach each other to soak cracked china in warm milk, to hope that the fissures may close.

It used to be, when a love wanted better from me, he would shout that I was *selfish.*

My mother's mother began her days frying bacon for her husband before she would wake him, with one baby girl or another pressed to the breast of her silky robes.

Wedgwood marketed china so that the desire for it spread from the queen to English high society to the rest of the country and then to America and, through generations, to my grandmother, who, before her marriage, began collecting it.

A china set includes, of course, cups and their accompanying saucers. Additionally, there are dinner plates and the chargers they can be placed on, salad plates, smaller dessert plates, and even more diminutive plates the size of pats of butter (quite different from lidded dishes for the whole stick), round bowls for soups, and ovals especially for sorbet, to name a few pieces. So many ways to serve.

▲

The number of items in a china set, each one's specialization, lessens the occasions for an individual's use. The multiplicity comes down to singleness of purpose, reduces the probability of being broken.

And if cracked china is soaked in milk, the protein may be some help in filling the space, but it's really by the clay's own natural sealing properties that it is healed.

A psychologist has said *selfish* is a word employed by those who wish to exert their own selves over another. Usually, it's a charge a man levels at a woman, speaking of what others might call having *expectations* or *ambitions*.

When my grandmother acquired china, developed a taste for its *translucent fired body*, I doubt she had my grandfather's pleasure in mind. Perhaps she was thinking of the future. I am now her collection's owner.

I don't much care for housekeeping, am more interested in how poetry has survived, though it is delicate, travels overseas and centuries. Still, each time I move, in addition to boxes of books, I pack the china carefully, wrapping it in the softness of my negligees. Protecting those gilt edges, which hedge against too much washing.

But after I unpack the stuff from the nightgowns that are too fancy to wear, I don't touch it, don't carry it, to the table, to anybody. Not even on the nights when it is my turn to make a meal.

I don't think my grandmother would mind that the lid of the sugar bowl has not been lifted or the creamer made to pour out anything in years. She turned that bacon in the pan with her bare hand. And she chose to save to purchase an egg coddler, a knife rest.

I do think of others. Here I offer an image on display: a pitcher that sits on the shelf, that does not have to be filled, even with a flower to make it appear a vase, to hold anything more than itself.

A LILY IS A LILY IS A LILY

1.

Not lily of the valley, not the trout, spider, water, peace, or calla lily—none of these are a true lily. Not even the daylily is deemed a true lily, though its blossoms, like the true lily's, are trumpets that blow out into stars. Not being true means that taxonomists have not included these plants in their invention, the genus *Lilium*.

At Easter, we hunted eggs in my mother's garden. At Valentine's Day, we sent bouquets to each other at school. We celebrated every occasion, both birthdays for sixteen years, together.

Lily is the name of my cousin. We grew up like sisters—or that's what we said.

Though we did not have the same genes.

▲

The daylily was the most abundant ornamental in the landscape of my childhood in the southern mountains. Only as an adult did signage in a city park planting tell me that the daylily is nearer, hereditarily, to asparagus than the bloom so mythically lovely it was the envy of Venus. That the daylily is not the pure flower said to have sprouted from Hera's breast milk, that it is not true at all.

▲

How to tell a true lily apart from an another?

A true lily has six petals, while a daylily has three petals and three sepals in disguise.

In a little time, Lily, sunbathing, lay back under the weight of breasts, hair and body blonder and bronzing. While my pallor blushed, all my matter stretching, angular, up into legs.

A novice may think the distinction between sepals and petals is insubstantial, but a seasoned botanist discerns it.

Lily could speak to our differences before either of us could write. When someone praised my dark curls, Lily said of her yellow ponytail, *Mine is silky*, lisping the *S* but articulating contrasting virtue.

2.

The calla lily is not only called a false lily but termed a *false flower*. The starched swirl that skirts its center doesn't have the characteristics of a petal—resists drooping, bruising, and shattering.

▲

There's the tradition of the gauzy white bridal gown with a train the bride's maids are supposed to carry above the dirt, if she is to reach the altar immaculate enough. A delicacy friends cultivate in the betrothed, according to the stories we're told, because they are being kind, they want her to shine on her special day.

And teenagers emerge from boutiques' fitting rooms modeling clothes and discarding them in piles according to whether the others say, *That's so last year, That's played out,* schooling each other in ephemeral beauty.

▲

Hey, don't copy me, poseur, the teenagers also declare, appraising each other's clothes. Or, *That doesn't look like you.* Suggesting individual, lonely styles.

And the bride, because she has beaten the other women to finding a mate, can expect them not to wear white, to differentiate themselves from her. It is also customary that the dresses they wear are not fancy enough to compete with the bride's for notice.

▲

I dressed in Lily's hand-me-downs as a child. They were good enough for a second wearer or needed only patches on the knees.

Lily did not marry young, did not marry until she'd become a sensible woman. For her wedding, she wore a knee-length shift and boots. After the ceremony, she, the rest of the bridesmaids, and I went for a walk through the woods behind her in-laws' house.

▲

The calla lily is characterized as insufficiently perishable, a ditch-clogging invasive, here, in the United States. But had people not imported it out of its native habitat, there would be no reason to call the flower domineering, a weed.

3.

The peace lily is often encountered on receptionists' desks and in the lobbies of medical facilities. Peace lilies require only low light and are low maintenance enough to survive almost anywhere, so they're generally considered nothing special. And accomplished growers have little interest in tending to them.

I've been spending plenty of time waiting for doctors. I have a condition that has been stiffening me since my thirties and could make my spine ossify, even as I am alive.

▲

At the culmination of hospital stays, on the ultimate occasions—deaths— pricey oriental lilies are sent to show deep sympathy.

▲

A peace lily is good for one function, an indoor plant expert suggests: serving as a canary in the coal mine of a greater potted collection, to indicate when the rest are about to need irrigation. Peace lilies are *expressive plants*: They wilt quickly and dramatically and can be restored easily with a bit of water. They are of interest when they suffer.

There would be a 50 percent chance of passing on the sickening antigen if I had a child, and it increases by various percentages the likelihood the child would develop numerous additional diseases. My back's predisposition to bow, shoulders to slope, and pelvis to degenerate means I won't be the one to carry a baby who will convey our family traits into the future.

But as far as we know, nobody else in my healthy family has the antigen I have. What happens to me says nothing about impending danger for others' offspring.

▲

Oriental lilies are also sent for births—cut flowers meant as symbols of life, ended or just at its fragile beginning.

▲

After hospitals failed our grandmother, well-wishers sent stargazer lilies to her funeral.

She had always referred to Lily and me as *her girls*, jointly, like one creature. And though our parents are different, in our relationship to her we were equal. It didn't occur to me to care that there weren't roses on her coffin. Lily and I held hands in the night-dark chapel.

4.

Female animals are unlikely to compete violently like males, whose function is to inseminate someone, because females' biological purpose is to stay alive to care for the offspring.

But there are means other than physical blows. *Armaments* are what animal bodies will have if females compete physically. *Ornaments* are what their bodies will have if they compete for mates more through appearances.

Plants have their ways of competing with each other: Flowers' showy shapes and colors vie to attract pollinators, markings guiding the way in to nectar to feed them. The lily has got its stellar petals, its beauty mark spots and its contrasting throat, cupping sweet syrup.

But plants' thorns and thick skins and bitter tastes aren't to protect them from members of their own kingdom. The lily's toxin is a response to insects' unwanted attentions, only sickens creatures that would eat it leaves and all.

▲

Plants can crowd and throw shade on each other, hogging the soil or open air.

But they also share water through networks, support their fellow *Plantae* in dry spells.

▲

Some female animals ostracize others, driving them from the flock or herd.

Occasionally, an animal may commit infanticide by stealing a baby and keeping it from the real mother until it dies of dehydration.

▲

Some female animals, if they are advanced *Homo sapiens*, choose this behavior: to cultivate ornamental flowers and invite guests to walk through their gardens, pointing away from their bodies toward what they can agree is gorgeous.

A female human, if she is not much of a gardener, may gather as much language as she can about lilies and arrange it prettily on the page because she wants to give it, the pleasure of reading, to others.

5.

The daylily spreads, the density of its green filling in bare roadsides and covering eroded creek banks. That's why it's also referred to ungenerously by some as the ditch lily. It does not need humans to give it anything, self-propagates, undiminished.

Daylily rhizomes travel on their own, and the tubers mass and multiply, allowing a woman to divide off a start and give it to a friend. On her land, the plant can continue offering bud after bud. So, all summer, spoken from the newest throaty flare to open, there can be an answer to the criticism that the daylily, a bloom lasting one day only, is shorted-lived.

I have a new reason to think of roots continuing. Lily has become mother to a baby girl.

▲

The lily of the valley, connected by fibers beneath the earth's surface to its colony, fends for itself on the forest floor. Or rather, they succor themselves, many bells nodding in agreement on every shoot.

This is the hardy flower I wish I could have sent to Lily on the day of her daughter's birth, when virus and quarantine orders prohibited visitation by all but next of kin.

Lily has named the child Hannah Rose, in that way shared her.

6.

The trout lily grows in the mulched margins between buildings and trees outside my office door and on the mountain where Lily and Hannah Rose's cabin sits.

Mostly, I will not be where they are. They have stayed in the state we are from. I have moved away, following my field. Which means nothing pastoral, only a decent job.

▲

The trout lily—also called the dogtooth violet—doesn't seem to care for formalities, with its wrinkled leaves lying low in the leaf litter. Call it the name of either of two types of plant, compare it to a slippery aquatic creature or a domestic terrestrial being—it is like many things.

My disease's name is so complex, I haven't learned to spell it. But never mind that. Hannah Rose has learned to write an *H*. Soon enough, she'll progress through the letters and reach the *R*.

7.

Among the few qualities people manage to fault true lilies for are their dark pollen and strong scent.

The early bloomer girl turns heads, gets noticed when she enters a room, and is the object of desire briefly. But girls are supposed to be quiet and tidy and leave few traces of what they do. Soon the ideal shifts to the woman who can stay thin. She's called the beauty because she can nearly disappear.

In middle age, perhaps my body, which can get closer to skinny than some, is a preferred type—in terms of looks (not procreation or other functions). But why think this way?

▲

A breeder of a new type of true lilies—called Rose Lilies—advertises, *We have cultivars with 12, 18, or 24 petals instead of the usual 6. What's more, they have no fragrance and produce no pollen. No headaches and mess for you.*

But I was drawn to read the ad because I was thinking of whom I miss. I wanted pollen and scent. I wanted the perfume to follow me into my home and add its aroma, its complexity, to the spices of the dinner my husband prepared. If I brushed against a flower, I wouldn't mind the turmeric-colored pollen mark, the reminder, on my finger.

8.

Among primates, if one female is attacked by another, usually grand-daughters and mothers and sisters and daughters will fight in her defense. But for evolutionary reasons, animal cousins are too distant to stand up for, and allegiance to friends doesn't usually exist. Females are pitted against all others but those who can most directly pass on the same genes.

I don't think there are equivalents to cousins, aunts, and nieces among plants. With flowers, it seems less clear whose offspring is whose, in the dense vegetation of an ecotone, or where the seed with its tiny propeller has flown or a rodent has transplanted a tuber.

▲

It is a comfort to see features similar to my aunt's and mother's appear on Hannah Rose's less-and-less-of-a-baby face. As some faces wrinkle and cave, the child's will fill out.

▲

I can interpret nature in ways that bolster my spirits and choose which components to make my similes. The fall of leaves at the end of the season feels much more acceptable if I think of them as related to spring, their rotting compost to feed seedlings.

A female monkey whose infant is killed may help with suckling and caring for the troop's remaining young.

9.

Another lily native to the place where Hannah Rose will be raised, the place Lily has returned, a place I recall so dearly, is the Turk's-cap. It's a tall figure dangling with as many as forty blossoms, which are vivid orange and dotted with darkness.

Its pattern reminds me of the matching leopard leotards Lily and I wore for Halloween. This was early on, when I was still padded with baby fat and she was the slenderer one, and those were the differences that others must have observed. Qualities that, at the stage, must have made her appear much more mature.

The Turk's-cap may be confused with the tiger lily, but the tiger lily is Asian, from another hemisphere altogether.

▲

When we had those costumes on, I just thought we were of a litter. Now, looking at a snapshot of us trick-or-treating, I still don't think this is an image in which Lily's shape, hinting at the teen age it will briefly be, shows our diverging futures.

I see my juvenile potbelly predicting what's ahead. Looking like her stomach swelled in pregnancy. And like, though I'll bear no children, most women eventually will look. We'll thicken around the middle as we get older, settling into our corpora, this earth.

▲

What does the Turk's-cap or tiger lily classification clarify anyway? Spots aren't what decorate a tiger's fur, and Turkey, to which our endemic's nomenclature refers, is a place so distant none of us have been there—yet.

The spider lily found wild in the Caribbean is native to West Africa. Some members of the genus's ancestors rode the part of the former continent Gondwana when it broke off and drifted away across the ocean.

Maybe Hannah Rose will go farther abroad than I ever did.

▲

Of course, plenty of plants also have limited ranges. The Columbia lily looks a lot like a Turk's-cap to me, but it lives in only one county in Montana.

Philopatry is the tendency to remain in the location of one's birth. Members of certain populations are supposed to do that; they don't require expansion into a new place.

Maybe Hannah Rose will stay in our home region for all the time she's given.

10.

A taxonomist has written that water lilies have less in common with true lilies than they do with the earliest, least-evolved plants. There's a dismissiveness to the tone. But through the ages, the water lily has stayed on, being itself, not changing, just regenerating.

And I remember well how Lily and I swam in a pond with water lilies when we were girls. We kept diving back in—in summer, into the evenings, until we were summoned for bed. In our joy before we were put to rest, in our saggy bathing suits with no one looking at us, we took pleasure in both the jumping and the paddling, we were not aware of our bodies as better than one element or another or of earth as apart from the heavens.

The roots of the water lilies were in the dirt we had just come from. The pads floated in the liquid by which we were held. The flowers curved up in a transcendent gesture, in the air where we next would travel.

REMAINS TO SEE

My father has collected the most substantial body of fish-based Index of Biotic Integrity data for a watershed of its size anywhere in the world. This is an accomplishment he can claim.

Though there are too many dull, qualifying words inserted between the superlatives beginning and ending the description of what he's done—or at least that's what I think.

He conducts his study in one North Carolina county (the county he's made his home). Every summer, he returns to the same sites he's visited for decades. He sinks an electric shocker's probes into the streams and nets the dozens of fish that float from the bottom, stunned.

But I want to describe this as spectacularly as the real thing. He conjures metallic, alchemical slivers. Their upturned bellies flash, surprising—the white of revelation.

He names black redhorse, golden redhorse, redbreast sunfish, green sunfish, greenfin shiner, yellowfin shiner, whitetail shiner, mirror shiner, smoky dace, rosyside dace, setting them free from the catchall of *minnow*. Such a vocabulary.

I've envied that language, trying to follow after him, wading through creeks as he does his surveys. I am small help with bucket or net, my hands fluttering between shading my sunburning skin and my gauzy version of note-taking. The notes are for poetry—that's what I write.

He examines and counts fish as tolerant or intolerant, as omnivores, piscivores, or herbivores. He tallies their lesions, diseases, and anomalies. He takes pages of field notes, making marks for each specimen in columns of waterproof paper.

How many columns per page? How many rows of pencil strokes in each of those? Hatch marks forming fences in their little sections of five—what all do they hold? He describes with numbers. He has these, in addition to language's powers.

The most substantial, in the world—these are phrases for his body of data. What he has achieved could cast too great a shadow for a successor to live in. However, I recall my father's work is driven by devotion to the small. He distinguishes between aquatic creatures most perceive only as shimmers on the pebbles below, as of lesser matter than the liquid through which they move.

I must put in perspective his remark that, had I been a fish, he would have thrown me back. (I was that little of a baby, premature, kept in an incubator so my lungs wouldn't explode.) He wants the delicate to survive, for there to be streams cool and clean enough for intolerant species to multiply.

He considers the findings from each stream each year, the differences in contrast to the past. Sometimes a change in fish population indicates a pollution source that can be determined (unfenced cattle causing bank erosion, a factory's waste treatment malfunctioning), and a demand for its cessation can be made. It is a possibility that the influence of planting shade trees or removing impediments to a stream's flow will yield visible results within the lifetime of the caretaker, and he will experience the thriving of rare and fragile creatures under his waters. But there are no guarantees.

My father does not expect all of the information will all be put to concrete, practical use. He values knowledge for the sake of knowing, information as testimony to observation, to the practice of attention.

Neither does my father expect to be here to witness his data applied. He notes as much as he can, understanding that one cannot predict which site's information will be needed in the future, or what kind. One cannot predict in advance how a stream will change, what will be illustrated through comparison to preceding conditions. His is a project for generations.

He keeps at work, though he is in his eighties. I keep spending my efforts on words that do not bear the weight of *threatened* or *endangered* (protective designations to which he may contribute), spend my time pursuing metaphors and rhyme.

The man of science has not always been sure of what to say to the poet, to the girl, the perplexity of what has been born of him. Yet to a reporter, I have heard him explaining: *You begin something. The good it turns out to be remains to be seen.*

True, more drafts than not I throw away. Maybe the wrinkles from squinting (to shield pupils whose blue irises are too pale to handle the light they're shown) will form my lines at their best. But I will keep looking—this much I can promise. And this much I will express: admiration of the wide-eyed sight of fish, their lidless vision, which does not end, even when at rest.

YOUR LOT

Maybe you are the kind of person who, in the state's early years, in the Georgia land lottery, drew lot 163: *Fertile land, one corner touches the Chattahoochee River.*

Maybe you got the house in the neighborhood with no bars on the doors, school district with high test scores.

Maybe your kind drew lot 114: *Entire lot a steep slope; no water.*

Maybe the house you can afford has lead pipes or paint or you come from a line of renters, never enough money for a down payment, no chance to change that predestination.

Maybe your ancestors were Creek, driven from the land, not allowed to keep an acre.

Maybe your family has no history here at all, didn't register on even nineteenth-century books, when seized land was redistributed, and now you hope to forge your connection by wandering around archives taking notes.

Maybe you can see the argument for the Georgia land lottery being egalitarian, redistributing land from the gentry, favoring veterans and their orphans, allowing even, in the terms of the time, *idiots, lunatics, widowed women and illegitimates,* a draw.

Maybe you are the kind of woman who makes planters out of trashed tires, uses discarded bottles to decorate trees, or the kind who tries to make something poetic out of the mess of history. *Lunatic, idiot, illegitimate,* do the sounds in those words have any music to find?

BETWEEN STATES

He Is Risen signs go up in the neighboring yards, making sure I remember Easter.

On Easter in 1865, Union troops attacked Columbus, Georgia, the city closest to my current address. This was the Civil War's last battle and useless. The Confederates had surrendered in Virginia already, but this far south, neither side knew.

On Easter more than a dozen years ago, I quit painting the window frames of the house I'd just bought with tape still all around the panes. I went to an Easter party and met a man who, within the year, would ask me to marry him.

This Easter, I'm setting up house for the sixth time, in a small town in Georgia. I'm pulling weeds, clearing overgrown vines that slow the passage along the walkway to, or from, the door.

▲

The Easter party happened when I had yet to leave the North Carolina mountains, where I was raised, a high part of the South where the cold lingers. The gathering was at a farm, outdoors. Little girls in white dresses ran around with white legs turning blue.

In that remote mountain county, locals like to claim their predecessors were so isolated that they had no stake in the Civil War, would change allegiance depending on which troops were closer. Even if this were true, there's no way for a white person to get around guilt, get out of being the part of our nation's culture that they are.

There are only strategies, unreasonable in varying degrees, for divorcing yourself from troublesome preceding events and carrying on.

Anyway, back in the true mountain climate, we needed a fire. And that's why, before we spoke, I had watched the man I would love using a wheelbarrow to carry a towering load of firewood over a pasture. When he encountered stobs, the remains of cut saplings, he'd draw back a little and push forward much harder and faster. In the first image of him my mind gathered, he is crashing on, over the obstacle.

▲

He set to tending the flames, elevating the temperature. I drew near, and his first remark to me was that the rivets in his pants were hot. And with that, thawing hastened, we, our rush of feeling, began.

We heard what might have been church bells, though they would have had to travel miles to get there, and he told me he'd been raised in a religious family. Then, how he'd been taught to say, when desire for a woman's body threatened, *Get behind me, Satan.*

As I stood in front of the fire, center of his view, he said what he'd chosen was to turn his back to that lesson.

Why cling to a tradition or other old thing you don't need?

▲

Who chooses the Lost Cause? Here people who still speak of the War of Northern Aggression and fly the flag of the Confederacy do. Dixie was defeated, and then the defeat was repeated, and yet—

Who is so ignorant as to believe there's reason to put up those *The South Will Rise Again* banners I see?

Here, in the conflictingly named Pine Mountain Valley where I now reside, the *Mountain* part of the nomenclature barely fits. Though any of it is better than how the place was known before: Chipley. Chipley, the surname of a railroad tycoon who was a Klan member, never convicted but thought to have been among the murderers of a progressive, *Negro sympathizer* judge.

The past: How is it that so many have so long managed to think of it proudly?

▲

Those years ago, I left the house that was mine unfinished and went to a party. I met a man who soon moved into my home and insulated the walls. I propped the door open—for his wide-roaming dogs.

Then I decided I was not ready to settle and asked him to leave.

Then he died.

And he did not rise.

▲

Now I've moved to another house. Where there's work, which happens to be farther south. Where he did not paint the beadboard, using my smallest watercolor brush to get into each groove.

I've married another man.

I try to be good, or better. My husband deserves devotion. But I'll never join the church folk like they keep asking.

I can't abide the other signs with which my saved neighbors adorn the eroded roadsides, printed in red with, *He died for your sins.*

▲

I did a lot of digging and burying when I first arrived, landscaping, adding perennials. There was dirt packed into my cuticles, every finger wrinkle, the setting of my ring. For a while, it seemed my hands were dirty all the time.

I suppose the born-again and those whose faith never wavered can tolerate telling the story of their Savior's killing every year because of the fresh feeling of conviction it arouses in them.

I don't mind *He Is Risen* so much. The phrasing *will rise* would set up an impossible hope. As a verb, *rose* is done and dull. So is *has. He Is Risen,* with its flawed grammar, offers at least the truth of the conflict between past and present tense.

Will the roots take and shoots sprout, will the flowers be beautiful next spring? I don't know. But I go out early, before the heat—heat's the problem in this region. I bring water to the starts, or the holes where plants should be.

FRAGMENTAL;
OR, ROCKS PRONE TO FRAGMENTATION
CREATE SOILS THAT ARE GOING
TO ERODE

—after *Let Us Now Praise Famous Gullies: Providence Canyon and the Soils of the South,* by Paul S. Sutter

Barren

Soil . . . is the one resource that can't be exhausted; that can't be used up, the agricultural expert had said. And landowners kept plowing, never rotating or resting their fields. A school fell into a gulley, then a church. In the 1930s, as much as an acre of Georgia per day crumbled and washed away.

I didn't know so much costly information could be put into a single brief sentence, a scientist later replied.

▲

What are the landmark sentences of a personal history?

I hear the gynecologist's voice—*She can take a real pounding*—while slipping into anesthesia for the procedure with effects I can never awaken from.

▲

When the earth could no longer bear, the opining turned, as judgments often do, to implying the virtues of the untouched and unused.

Leading men put forth explanations that were not their exploitation of the land. What had started the gullies was a path wild animals or Indians had worn long ago. No, it was a woman—the problem had originated at the point where she threw out dishwater. Over and over, she did the too familiar work, until she ruined the dirt.

Attraction

Gullies 150-foot-deep expose several million years of sedimentary layers, reaching to levels deposited during the age of the dinosaurs and then baring even lower, outside Lumpkin, Georgia. These incisions in the land did not exist until twentieth century, would not have appeared were it not for agricultural erosion.

The gullies a revelation. But a sundering by humans, not God's will done.

The land's bodice ripped open. Or more like a garment's zipper jerked down too hard to ever be able to close its rough teeth again.

Georgians lobbied for this site to be designated a national park and were unsuccessful, outsiders deeming it more of a human-made disaster than a natural wonder. So locals named it Providence Canyon and made it a state park.

And now tourists come—call it an *attraction.*

Junk cars bear signs identifying them as wildlife habitat. A photographer takes wedding portraits against the roseate-shaded walls of dirt, backdrop the ivory-attired bride must not be touched by. Mothers and fathers close the spaces between themselves in embraces long enough for family vacation pictures.

I've brought my love to see this view.

The combination of sand and clay that compose the landscape continues to change and erode. The term for such mixed soils is *incompatible.*

Making the best, accepting what you've got—are these the problem or the things worth seeing here? The young woman in stilettos maneuvers over, an older woman tells her child about the geological uniqueness of, this shifty earth.

Like Rivers

Some people are buried at the top of the hill, where the grass is mown weekly by the town. They have engraved granite and obelisks above their heads and petite iron fences staking out plots, are not ready to cede property even in death.

Some people are buried at the back and bottom of the hill, graves covered in vines with no stone or marker other than rectangular indentations, the shapes of where coffins had been, bodies gone on.

▲

West Georgia, in an aerial view, is greener, more forested, now than at the time of the Civil War.

Trees and shrubbery in the Deep South often indicate, not places conserved, but where cotton plantations failed and ceased to be. The population is a fraction of what it was because people are no longer bound by enslavement or sharecropper's indenture here.

▲

When it rains this evening, the runoff and flowers from the top of the hill will be swept to the bottom. The slight hollows that are the lower graves will be filled with water and, with silk and plastic petals added to wild honeysuckle blooms, they'll be doubly festooned.

This isn't any sort of justice, just an image to carry thoughts downstream, toward picturing possibility someday, past hard things.

▲

The geological materials of the region are inclined to fracture, and similar agricultural uses farther North would not have had such an impact.

Still, what did, was permitted to, happen in the South was King Cotton, his subjugating reign, his washing the richness of the topsoil away.

▲

The *rock record* is the term for what humans use to measure geologic time.

But look beyond rocks: Geologic time scrapes clean, wears away, whatever is piled, hoarded, elevated in little mounds. Water follows the plan written by grade and gullies, off toward rivers that overcome by carving deeper, engraving lasting lines.

Eye

To look away can be to spare the self. To look away can be a danger, a denial.

To be stone blind is to lack perception completely. To be stonehearted is to lack all sympathy.

I have a house on a mountain, where a quartzite deposit has endured while the surrounding sandy soils have been weathered flat. I have a view down onto the town but turn toward the forest.

I have looked away from others. Though the men who frighten me look away from my face to stare at my body. I have looked away like the doctor who harmed me, a fellow woman who, after the botched surgery, could not meet my gaze. I look away from devastations vaster than mine, which I cannot see a way to repair.

But also, in stone, there may be eyes (formations called *augen*, from *eyes* in German). There may be clusters of hard minerals that curve to tapered ends, and these exist amid softer layers, are a part of metamorphic history.

But also, I have been taught one should avert the eyes when another cries, to give them that grace. I have tried to learn to find, so I can show, the good in things—the textural details and sparkling veins.

In stone walls, masons leave weep holes to allow stormwater to pass through, so what they've built will yield and not fall. Stone walls do not stop, do not refuse the rain's flow. They are not dry, they are not closed.

(UN)DISCLOSED

Period. End punctuation. Finality.

First menstrual period, No bad results.

First menstrual period, Natural.

These entries appear in orphanage papers from the 1800s, are the final sentences about their residents. That's it, all they or the reader get. Periods are the conclusion of the girls' childhoods and signs that soon there will be no place for them, as young women, in the institution. The keeping of their short records is done.

It's the start of when they can become mothers.

For years, I have been waiting to adopt a child. That is why I've been digging through archives of an orphanage that used to stand near my home.

I'm having to make do with history. What I want is to move into the future, where my daughter exists, in my imagined, beyond-the-horizon view.

▲

Agency reports on birth mothers who may consider me as an adoptive parent for their babies provide summaries of their physical health. Also a brief questionnaire.

It was answered as follows, by E., a mother placing her child for adoption in 2023, after finding she was pregnant at eight months and one week:

Insurance provider? None

Prenatal care? Not yet

What is your highest degree? GED

Relationship to the father? Not involved

How do you like to wear your hair? Short

What is your favorite color? Brown

What is your favorite thing about yourself? _____

The author of the form is a full-grown woman. It is over a century after the orphanage was shuttered. Yet the mother does not provide much more of a story than is available from the girls' papers. The incompletion gapes.

▲

Another birth mother names pink as her favorite color. I make too much of the little personal difference between liking brown and pink, trying, and failing, to manufacture full characters.

On the questionnaire given to me, I can specify the sex of the child I prefer and the ethnicities I will not accept. I write *female,* then leave a blank of my own. There is little I will control—nothing she experiences in utero, nothing in her DNA's code.

▲

Three periods can be arranged into an ellipsis—which indicates trailing uncertainty, indecision, omission, the phrases edited out of the quotation.

V., age thirteen, and F., age seven, are noted as adopted in the asylum records. Then, one line and one month later, noted returned. An ellipsis is all I could write to suggest what I suppose might have happened in the home of the adopter, Mr. B. That information kept discreet.

▲

Her period was normal the whole time—she was shocked to find out that the pain she was experiencing was labor.

The first sentence in the background report on C., another woman placing her infant for adoption in 2023.

What did she not let herself know, what feelings and swellings and measures, in the months before being taken to the emergency room, did she omit?

▲

Formative periods are those the mind, the memory, the biographers, return to.

My girl may, today, be no more yet than an egg among the hundreds of thousands deep inside a person whose face I couldn't recognize. I carry my girl loosely, as a dreamy idea, still free to cleave, differentiate, hatch, grow.

▲

The gestational period forms the body.

Yet of course, the body keeps on growing after. Infants with low birth weights, given extra early care, catch up with peers before any can speak sentences in full.

▲

The only other facts in the notes on the nineteenth-century orphans are medical: *Mumps serum, measles serum. Vaccinated for small pox. Inoculated against whooping cough. Ringworm, treated. Bed wetting, improving.*

Contemporary birth mothers' form fields tell their age, height, weight, and race. Checked boxes indicate whether they are right- or left-handed; glasses wearers or not in need of eye correction; and fair, medium, olive, or dark complected. Not divulged are their last names, locations, or other identifiers.

The documents reduce their subjects. Yet should I be permitted, wish, to uncover more?

There were no further medical records because the girls' treatments were complete. When they were eighteen, they were of age, free, ready to try to find houses that they did not have to sign a register to enter or leave.

I'd like to believe the birth mothers have new starts, schools and jobs, moves and loves ahead. I try to believe some of them just demurred on the forms, thought better of themselves than the blanks suggest.

▲

There are waiting periods. Grieving periods. The expectation is to get through.

Periods are ends, but beginnings are supposed to be involved too. For instance, the Archaic period ended, then there was the Classical period in art, its restrained, graceful forms.

▲

I will know little of my daughter's origins. My concern is where girls and women may yet go.

Whatever is next created—some circular thing, some looping in, continuing on—I believe it requires no sharing of blood.

A DOOR IS A THRESHOLD IN WHICH
YOU CAN TURN EITHER WAY

For centuries, to enter or lock a door involved lifting bars of wood or drawing strips of leather. Doorknobs were a major evolution. With one motion of twist and push, requiring only one hand, they grant admission to rooms.

I came upon this information, a surprise, while I was trying to find antique doorknobs, or reproductions at least. I wanted glass rosettes with stars bezeled in their hearts to install in the new home I'd bought with my husband. I wanted them to look like the knobs in the first house where I'd lived, which were so old the spindles fell from the holes.

Doorknobs continued to evolve, moving from their positions mounted in the middles of doors to the right sides, as has now become customary. This update was made with the thought of leverage away from the hinge rather than beauty and the harmony of centering.

When I tried to write about doorknobs, I worried that the essay couldn't just be centered on inanimate objects, had to have a second, metaphorical meaning. That the piece had to skew more toward me, if anyone was going to be interested. That for nonfiction to be deemed creative and appeal to the emotions, it must bare something personal to the reader.

Doorknob phenomenon is a term describing the behavior of a patient who so wishes to keep the paper gown closed to the doctor, her embarrassment unspoken, pent up, she does not reveal the reason for the appointment. Until his hand rests on the knob, has turned it halfway, and himself, toward the exit. Then she will tell.

This should go without saying: No one should have to feel such shame. I will say it plainly anyway, to be clear.

Perhaps, according to the tastes of the day for disclosure and exposé, I should have admitted already how, long ago, a stranger pulled the door to the room where I was sleeping to seal the opening behind him. And in the levered handle's click of latch plunging past the faceplate, through strike plate, into borehole, I heard portent of what would occur—

But I do not want to give my words to that man or make them answer to other demands. I do not want what happened that one night to be the point I am continually thinking toward. And I do not want to reveal more. What's intimate is intimate because most people aren't let in.

My love and I didn't change anything about the locking exterior doors. What we did manage was to fit glass passage knobs throughout the interior of our house. We attached them securely, the pegs aligned.

I don't feel there's need for further progression after the knob. Some install push doors, which encourage users to slam and shove them, or electric models that slide open at any motion, leaking cold air. But the same round hardware has long served well. I suppose a sphere is harder to grapple with than some other forms. But loyalty to the familiar must stop the forward press somewhere.

It's time for bed, for going into our room and closing the door. For the clasp of partners' arms, the hasp of entangled legs. And then for sleep, the hands relaxing their grasps, though keeping a curved, cupped shape.

A GOOD POUR

The airport bartender says she works in an airport because she doesn't want regulars. I don't frequent airports because I like to walk the same quarter-mile of creek each evening and see tadpoles in the puddles again, the heron standing in the current. The Flint River originates under the Atlanta airport. The Atlanta airport has the most departures of any in the world. The tadpoles' lacy thin legs appear merely decorative, floating by their sides. The heron only ever seems to need one leg at a time, folding the other away. The airport requires forty-seven hundred acres of space. It is too far between the airport gates to walk, so passengers must crowd into subterranean trains. There is no room for the river; it is piped out of the way, down even lower than a subway. A person cannot, of course, take liquids or aerosols or gels through security. Having surrendered drinks, you must covet the other half of the can the flight attendant doesn't pour in your plastic cup, if you did not purchase water, or refill a bottle, queue-ing up to bow your head and bend your knees at fountains before takeoff. Most likely, you won't have time for a pause, to sit down for a meal at one of the airport's more than one hundred restaurants. Unless your flight is delayed and you are stranded and hungry for many hours, which is the other likelihood. In the food court kitchens, knives or any potentially dan-gerous tools must be tethered to cooks' workstations so no one can run in and grab them and force a pilot to crash a plane. So, some things do stay in place. And the river isn't contained utterly. The Flint emerges down-stream. Then fishermen catch big bass in it. Though the fish aren't safe for human consumption, due to pollutants, including antifreeze washed off from the airport runways. Air travel is a major player in melting the glaciers. What change are jetsetters seeking, is it just of scenery, what do they really want to see? The sea is rising and coming to us in our home ports. But I don't really want to critique the more adventurous with their light backpacks and quick-dry attire. In truth, when I've traveled, I've been embarrassed by my bad packing of suitcases I could barely close, how I always tried to cram in an entire wardrobe. I just want to point out what there is here at home that others find worth fighting for. Where the river flows southward, in locations landlocked and droughty, Florida and Georgia compete for rights to the resource, to pump it for irrigation. I just want to say that before the river gets to a state border, nearer my twelve acres of property, there's a slow stretch where rare lilies and relict trilliums bloom on the banks again every spring. And when I say *I'll have another* these days, I mean a glass of water.

SEVERAL SMALLER STONES

—after *Practical Stone Masonry Made Easy,* by Stephen M. Kennedy

The stone masonry book says, *Ideal assemblages can only be realized with cut stone. With rubble masonry utilizing found materials, these are just ideals.*

So: the dark but stars. The winter but bonfires. Blistering summer day and a siesta in its midst. A long commute from the office to a house in the forest. Economy car. Discovery in the discount bin. Camellias browning before the azaleas open. Laurels after daffodils. Never one without the other being over but still flowers. Waist thickening yet the legs beneath the floppy dresses slim. Tumor, copay, wait, noncovered, but not cancer, praise be. A friend who can monitor her diabetic daughter's glucose from overseas. No way to touch or tend the child but at least milligram and decimal readings that speak of blood and sugar.

Dry stacking a stone wall, rather than using mortar, allows the structure to freeze and thaw without cracking, to respond to changes in the earth.

How women in the Civil War substituted possum for chicken, gunpowder for salt. Like them, today trying vinegar in place of citrus, for sugar sorghum, stevia leaf, or pure imagination instead. The teacher pulling the rows of institutional desks in a circle. When the catalpa worms eat all the riverside catalpa tree's leaves and, fattened, fall into the water below, the fish feeding. And the fisherman wading over from his bank to cast a lure. The wish for a purebred hound, tall and leggy, guarding the door. Then the stray, who lays in grass reveling in the softness on her belly, came.

Instead of a larger perfect stone, you can use several smaller ones.

Mint leather lining in waterproof black boots, polka-dotted satin inside the gray wool blazer. A place for the Easter egg in the fence post or under a flower of the exact same color. Hummingbirds. During the phone call's long hold, counting tree frog toes pressed to the window. Boxes emptied of their first gifts, but cats pressing themselves into the cardboard's dimensions. A cousin's daughter, close enough to call her niece. Grandmother gone but the scent of powdery perfume lingering in her clutch purse. In the months between visits, mother's stitches holding up the hem and on the button.

Don't worry about a few gaps in a dry stacked wall. Light and shadows are pleasing to the eye, but cement usually is not.

Neighbor who knows better than to mention the election, anything beyond the weather and garden. The movement of creek water, of leaves in breeze, the perfectness of their irregularity, and how no scientific explanation makes nature's doings plain. Snaps that hold bras' straps to dresses'. By candle instead of lamp. Never stop closing the bathroom door, no matter how long you're married. No need to know who he remembers when his eyes go dreamy, if it's memory or wish. The storm door's extra layer of shelter in winter, in summer opening to the warm, with the screen door's filter.

My love finding stones in the surrounding woods, bringing them to our acres. Practicing balancing and fitting quartzite, dolomite, and schist together. Using gravity and a long *through stone's* weight to bind the pieces in their position. Walking from our house along the path we've worn. Thinking how I'd carry a child so it wouldn't seem too far to her, how I'd lift the ginger's heart-shaped leaves to show the pods called *pups* attached to the stem. Going out to be beside him. Reading what he reads.

On the first page, the book began with this advice for minimizing a project's difficulty: *Choose a site near a pile of rocks.*

REINTRODUCTION

An elk stands in frost that flashes like smashed glass.

Though I suppose the metaphor should be constructed with what came into the world later referencing that which existed first. So: Crashed cars' broken mirrors along the highway side possess something like the glitter of frost.

▲

The elk stands in the auto shop's parking lot.

Rather, the auto shop, the highway, and every house to which it could be followed have been built on what was elk territory before humans came, hunted them down, and by the 1800s, crowded them entirely out of the eastern side of the country.

▲

Reintroduction is what importing elk—to give them another try—is called.

Importing them from where they survived to where they were eliminated, where they would have never chosen to be absent from. *Reintroduction*—as if they are guests prone to forgetting names and must be led through the same handshakes all over again at each party they attend.

Today is the first time I've encountered an elk in my home state.

Also, today is my birthday. I've come home to visit my parents. It's late enough into life that the date has begun to feel more like an annual redundancy than time for a celebration.

Their numbers increasing beyond expectations, the elk are making great progress.

Ranging beyond the parkland they were given, the elk are already considered a problem. They are slowing traffic as they travel by road. The elk are coming down from the mountains to graze on grasses. And on corn on rare occasions.

Humans have written laws to provide protections. These say it is illegal to kill an elk.

However, if an elk is in a man's garden and he shoots it, he is unlikely to be charged with a crime or even an animal replacement fee. An exception to the law made because it was encroaching on his private property.

Animal replacement fees are supposed to compensate for the losses—of tax dollars and the pleasure of elk sightings—of the citizenry.

What impedes traffic, by the way, are cars of gawkers stopping as the elk continue to walk.

▲

These days, I run slow. I won't wear a watch to see how much longer the route takes me now than it did at another age.

What I want is to go back to past times, my knees high-stepping then. Or back further, to crawling on them. Maybe to push back human clearing and construction, sweeping error from the land. Though that would have to include my own family's home.

▲

This elk has pushed ahead beyond the rest of his kind to find territory another buck hasn't already claimed.

That is why he isn't a part of any herd. The trouble is, where there are no competitors of his sex, neither are there females. Only ground lonely as this is uncontested.

▲

Is there, in the spread of the elk yet to occur, reason to hope for what's ahead?

Think of the elk. Think several generations on, my body, already past its time for speed or breeding, entirely gone, when there has been time for more elk to wander here and fill in the space.

An elk's eyes perceive movement more than detailed shapes. I keep still. In his eyes, I can disappear by staying in place.

No, more than elk see anything, they rely on listening. I could describe myself as being at a *dead stop*. But I am still breathing, revealing myself in that way.

I remember many childhood birthdays with cakes, how I was shown I was welcome in this world with singing and flame, year after year. The candles as bright as the rays refracting from the frost now.

Day will melt the frost's beauty. But then there will be, again, the full, direct, and original light of the sun. And wouldn't most people be glad, shouldn't I be eager for the warmth, expect better to dawn yet?

I stare at the elk, standing by a highway with lanes to follow in either direction. I should believe that the way he is looking is to the future.

Or given what I know of elk's senses, I should say, more likely, he is listening for what's to come. Hearing the drum of a hooved harem running over the hills, the nearing of does.

NEGATIVE

—for my paternal grandmother, Catherine McLarney, née Gallagher

Nobody is putting another needle in me unless there's a bottle of gin at the end. That's what my grandmother said, according to the nurses who were there, when she was hospitalized in her nineties. She chose not to receive fluids and to die.

I must have given more than two thousand injections to my cat. Every day, for years, I kept him alive by inserting a needle in the skin of his back. We'd lie on the bed together for the ten minutes it took for a hump to fill with liquid to supplement his failing kidneys.

▲

At my unoccupied house, all that sits in the windowsill where the cat once sunned is a glass bottle etched with *Gallagher Prescription Druggist*. Gallagher was the maiden name my grandmother surrendered so long ago. It's a negative impression scratched, by a heavy steel needle with a handle like a pen, onto this empty vessel that light passes through.

Where I am is a tattoo parlor. I'm sitting holding sketches of a cat's shape on waxy paper, the design a gun will drum into my skin with its clusters of fine steel needles.

▲

People admired my grandmother's decision to die, and some may have thought her life was sad. (She'd been a widow forty years, hundreds of miles away from her one son and granddaughter.)

Likely people thought that I cared for my cat as I did because my family is in other states, I have few friends. (In addition to fluids, I administered pills and powders and creams, prepared a special diet for him too.) Probably they thought that it was regrettable how I let my feelings stray to a feline body—

In *Why Look at Animals,* John Berger wrote of humans' relationships with pets in our postindustrial age when we no longer encounter animals in nature or work beside them in agriculture. We make them possessions held within the walls of single-family homes, and, he says, *With their parallel lives, animals offer man a companionship which is different from any offered by human exchange. Different because it is a companionship offered to the loneliness of man as a species.*

Juan Ramón Jiménez wrote a book-length elegy for an animal companion (in this case a donkey), *Platero and I.* In the section "The Best Friend," while Platero still walks beside him, the speaker explains why he prefers to share his life with Platero rather than having humans as companions: *You give me your company and do not remove me from my loneliness . . . you allow me my loneliness without removing your company.*

▲

My grandmother stayed in her three-story Victorian house—in the town where her parents, friends, and husband had grown up and been buried—alone. She kept herself occupied with walks to the library to borrow and return books she held dear and were not hers to keep and Latin masses to attend for the comfort she found in that dead language.

And she busied herself with letters, which she wrote every week from the time of my birth to the time of her death. Weekly, without fail, they came from her northern end of the country, south to me.

▲

I had her letters for company when I was an only child in a rural county with no neighbors for miles around. When I went to college, to a bare little room, her letters arrived there, to the mailbox protected from the city by lock and key.

Later, when my first love left the home we had shared, the cat is what he left me with. The cat would catch reptiles and bring them in. A slender, cream-colored Oriental shorthair, with a black snake extending, contrasting, from either side of his mouth, he was a striking picture of the un-Edenic condition into which we'd fallen.

▲

My grandfather died well before I was born. My family was too poor to fly, my grandmother too old and set in her routines to travel, and so I saw her, when my father had time to make the long drive, at most once in a year.

The cat was my partner for almost twenty years, as other men, after the first, came and went in briefer stints. When I began to roam, the cat was under my seat on airplanes and beside me hitchhiking, a caterwaul escaping the carrier. He was a tongue that licked the hand I stuck in, soothing. Or a paw that scarred it with scratches, a part that, even when trying to break out of the box's confines, clung tight to my fingers.

▲

Tattoos are not a big deal these days, I know—they don't mark you as a bad girl or otherwise special.

But I'm not sure whether it makes me feel tougher or more out of my element when a man walks into the tattoo parlor and says that this is his first stop upon release from prison.

My grandmother's letters told of some of my grandfather's troubles, how he had been given a job at her family's drugstore, but as soon as her father sold it, the new owners fired him. Then, in what might seem a rejection of the party of health, he began working as an undertaker.

What she wrote was not the content everyone would share with children. She continues, in a letter in which she also inquires into what I am studying in the third grade, about the mortuary profession: *You may not realize it, but there is a great deal of artistry involved, particularly in accident cases. They work HOURS on the bodies.*

I don't deny that as a pet owner, I made a being dependent on me for survival and the decision about when his life would end. Yes, I participated in the practice of depriving animals of the ability to hunt food, neutering them, removing any source of interaction except the human.

And then I had my cat killed with another needle. I called a vet to come to the house and euthanize him on the hearth, where he was curled in my sweater, when he no longer had the ability to stand. All I can say in defense of what I've done as a pet's master is that the cat's death, in a familiar place, seemed kinder than many humans', solitary in hospitals.

▲

Another of my grandmother's letters included, *Your grandfather said, when he died, he wanted to be stuffed and mounted with his hand raised in greeting and displayed in a case in the entry hall.*

I am getting the tattoo on the inside of my right wrist so it will show when I reach my hand to take or offer something, to extend toward someone else's hand in introduction.

▲

The man just out from behind bars selects some skulls and smoke plumes for his tattoos—images of vanishing, demise.

But he cannot complete the tattoo parlor's releases because he has no photo ID. He has been stripped of who he is—or how a man is supposed to prove he is the kind of person society supposedly wants him to be—by our systems.

▲

My grandfather died of a heart attack in his fifties, though he was the boy who had announced that he intended to marry my grandmother when they were just eight and was supposed to care for her for decades more. After, my grandmother wrote that she sat in the hospital beside his body and said everything she hadn't yet had a chance to articulate. A reserved woman, she must have left a good bit unspoken, of which only the air of that temporarily assigned room may be aware.

Later she'd make a hard choice for herself, but first there had been this dying, this horrible surprise.

▲

I think of what I don't know, perched on the stained church pew that is the tattoo parlor's ironic waiting room seating.

While the man stares at the blanks in his paperwork.

▲

No member of my species will ever get closer to me than the cat was, no lover has been at my ankles at every step or would I let accompany me into the bathroom like my pet—there is no other presence I would miss at so many moments in every hour after I let him go. This should be taken not as a commentary on my loneliness or need but as a testament to depth of a love.

In the 1700s, Christopher Smart famously paid tribute to his cat Jeoffry in the rapturous "Jubilate Agno." He praises the cat as an *instrument to learn benevolence upon* and proclaims, *For he counteracts the Devil, who is death, by brisking about the life.* Smart writes of the cat's admirable qualities: of quickness and tenacity, kindness and elegance, his *mixture of gravity and waggery.* And centuries after, there is still much to love in this writing.

▲

A recent book by Louise Glück contains the lines *The little cat is dead, meaning, I suppose, / one's last hope . . . The cat is dead: who will press now, / his heart over my heart to warm me?* I used to say that Glück was the first influence on my poetry, and her acerbic work does resonate. But I've realized of late that I may have loved her words because they sounded like her predecessor's, my grandmother's.

My grandmother's final letter contained the observation *The music of to-day offends my aesthetic sensibilities, but not enough to get excited about it. I do not care for jazz as music. My taste runs to funeral dirges.* At least she was still thinking of music in the end.

I hear my grandmother's voice every time I write. I borrowed an austere, stern tone from her when I was young and not as sure of myself or anything as of her letters' arrival. She's the influence who made me an author.

I see my white cat, for an instant, in any corner where, at his height, there is a shaft of light.

The freed man is wearing white Air Jordans with an ironed white tee and white jeans, stunning against his dark skin. Someone must have excitedly bought and sent these for him to wear out into the world, pictured him immaculate. Or as they prepared this offering, did they think how small and momentary a piece of white clothing and its mint condition are, especially in the face of a history dirtied with injustice and the many more trials of daily life he will be subjected to ahead?

What did my grandmother see when she watched my grandfather working in the drugstore when they were young and he still had that job, where he was put behind the soda shop counter more often than the pharmacy's, as he scooped ice cream for children? As he admonished them to lick faster before it melted and rivulets stained their wrists, was it a picture of simple pleasure? Or of perishability, which she should start steeling herself to endure?

Once, when I awoke to a snowstorm and my cat missing. As I ran searching for him through the trees at night, I imagined that he had become the white suspended all around me. (On that occasion, in the morning, I found him sleeping by the heater. But it is in the vast air, if anywhere, that I feel the spirit of him, in perpetuity, resides.)

My grandmother left instructions that I was not to miss class to attend her funeral and a poem that was, unusually for her, conventionally sentimental: *Do not stand at my grave and weep. I am not there. I do not sleep. I am a thousand winds that blow. I am the diamond glints on snow.* I preferred her own original writing, but I obeyed. And I have yet to go back to visit her cold resting place. Afterall, she is not there. Or it does not matter where the physical remains lay.

Mine were sins of omission was another comment in my grandmother's correspondence. Weren't those sins—emotions she had not explicitly stated—in comparison to the alternative of active transgressions made, less grave?

I wish what I have to say was larger, mattered more, concerned those beyond my own relations.

▲

I wonder what happened while the man in the tattoo parlor was locked away, about the cultural events and familial moments, big changes and pleasantly routine things that he may have been forced to omit from his days.

He was quick to settle on stock drawings from posters on the parlor's walls for his tattoos—glad to be able to make any choice, I'd venture. But I shouldn't presume.

▲

My tattoo design is custom, commissioned and readjusted several times to better represent the angularity of the cat's head, the remarkable length of his body. And to show something of his vigor, how he'd soak up the heat stretched on my Carolina porch, climb the drapes of cheap interstate motels, sharpen his claws on the fir trees in the wilderness of the West Coast when we reached there. Though what I want to capture is an impossibility: wildness. And a fearlessness that, when I compared myself to him at the time, had made me feel like I, worrying over my suitcases and what I couldn't manage to bring, did not live experiences intensely enough.

The man and I exchange only nods, don't speak directly. I overhear him say that when he's able to afford another tattoo, he is going to get the entire ocean—waves and sharks and the creatures farther down—covering him. He won't be around here anymore when that happens (I won't get to see). But I observe that talking of this future is when he looks the closest to happy.

▲

I never met my grandfather. But he never seemed like a complete stranger, thanks to the letters. My grandmother's comments on the mortuary trade were not macabre; they were a defense of what my grandfather did, an expression of loyalty. They were written in the style by which I knew her, like some children know the feeling of their grandmother's hugs. And of course, my grandmother could not stuff and mount my grandfather's body as requested, retain his physical presence in the house. But what she could convey, which is a variety of keeping, was a sense of his humor, his stories.

The subject matter to which I am drawn is not so grim. The maudlin poet, that stereotypical role, is not one I want to fit in.

The writer making metaphors describes objects that are not exactly the subject, or her only one.

Animals do not share language with humans. But we owe them for it, Berger observes, and reference to them is in whatever we say. They were the first things we painted on cave walls, not images of ourselves. Animals were the source of symbols and led to figurative expression. Figurative, he argues, not direct speech, was our original kind of expression.

▲

The man in the tattoo parlor is not a metaphor for my grandfather, not to be used like an animal. He is someone whose appearance I portray because he is in front of me. My grandfather, a person I've never seen, is the one I may load with almost inarticulable feelings, I have more right to make him the beast of burden of my figurative meanings.

I tell the tattoo artist about the next tattoo I want done—a simple band of two lines around my left forearm. She tells me straight lines are the least simple element of a tattoo to execute. And to make lines run parallel is harder still.

▲

The artist practiced her craft on a substitute—by tattooing grapefruits.

I trained to give my unprofessional medical care—the subcutaneous injections my cat required—by stabbing needles through oranges' peels.

▲

My grandmother would have never come into a place like the tattoo parlor. If I am trying to memorialize her, how did I let my lines of writing end up here?

The tattoo artist says that if I want one of the two lines around my arm to be thicker, as I have suggested, if I want to give the one more emphasis and weight, she will actually have to tattoo that line once and then circle around above it again. She would actually have to tattoo three lines. Aligning even more pieces is even more difficult to achieve.

▲

The cats in today's tattoo are not so technically challenging. The overlapping sketches of the animal moving through different poses—climbing, standing, stretching, lying down—are flowing, more suited than symmetry to the natural inclinations of the hand.

My grandmother, by the way, quit keeping pets after my father went off to school, and though she may have admired cats' aloofly regal attitudes, I am not aware of her having a particular affinity to the species. I acquired my cat soon after her death and had him about as long as I received letters from her, but that's not a clear congruity either. There are figures that aren't themselves so defined. Yet by brisking at the edges of another's life, they give it shape.

▲

I tell the artist that when I return for my next tattoo, I will settle for the sparer version of two thin bands. I don't really care what's on the second arm. I just want something on the left side to balance out the right. After-all, the band design I've come up with primarily frames an area that is un-inked, between.

The pharmacists at Gallagher Prescription Druggist were said to have dispensed placebos, sugar pills and syrups, to those whose illness they did not deem true or more than could be withstood. Sometimes giving people what's not real (in typical understandings) is as effective as giving them a substantive thing.

▲

In the tattoo parlor, all I can do is look down at my book and try to grant the man privacy as he explains his situation to the shop owner at the register.

He needs the tattoos now because they will cover symbols inked on him while he was incarcerated. When he says this, the owner, understanding the associations from which the man should be released, concedes. The man and I are both taken to booths, and on the other side of the divider, he stays silent, never exclaiming at pain. I am glad I am able to keep quiet too, throughout the guns' whirring.

▲

The cat was a weight at the end of the bed, the feeling of whose landing I knew down to the gram. He was a presence whose leap and return I waited for, when he went exploring the night in which I could not see. Now there is no end to his absence.

My grandmother asserted her presence in my life on bone white—or, no, less substantial—ghostly, see-through paper. So I barely knew her as a body to mourn or learned to care much about the flesh. What we didn't have couldn't be lost.

▲

If my view is negative, let it be so in the way that space is.

Soon the man will be able to rise from the synthetic leather of the chair and disappear, out into what is—in the limits of my narrative, the perspective from this window—the anonymity of the crowded street.

MOUNTAIN MUSIC

When I parked at the high school, I'd back up the CD. I'd think ahead to departure, so a track I wanted friends to hear would start with my car. We lived in a rural county, and driving is what there was to do, me holding the CD player plugged into the tape deck, to steady it and lessen skipping on gravel roads. It didn't matter if the other high schoolers and I had any tastes in common; geography determined the few people to whom we could be close. We drove to talk or to tell each other to shut up when the good parts of a song came on. To not really focus on the Appalachian scenery tourists came to view while we tried to discern what we could from each other's expressions in profile. The lines of those features, and the ridges behind—

X. had pressed *play* and *fast forward* and *pause* and *record* to make the best mixtape I'd ever heard, but I didn't know about him until I'd listened to it for over a year. I borrowed the tape from my prom date, who'd gotten it from a friend, who'd gotten it from a friend, who got it from X. X. had graduated long enough ago that he'd had time to move away and come back with this music, Aphex Twin and Sonic Youth, with measures of pretty and hard that were marvelous to me, a dissonance I played with constancy. The kids my age called some of it pure noise. I forgave them for not getting it, not being cultured yet. *Pure noise* is a phrase I like still, for the idea that purity might be things crashing together.

When I finally met X., learned the tape had originated with him, he became my first true love. X. showed me how to match beats and scratch records on the turntables behind his mother's jars of green beans in the basement where he stayed. He took me across state lines to warehouse clubs, where he lifted me (not yet eighteen) over the back fences. I re-member one night, as I waited for him to make his way through the door and bouncers, standing at the edge of those pogoing for the band I'd come to see, I watched two drag queens dance over from the adjoining venue. They formed hearts with their hands that they beat at each other. Their gesture, unlike the fist pumping with which I was familiar, still converged into a shared romantic affair.

X.'s uncle had a game camera trained on the creek that played into the kitchen, not to spot deer but to funnel in the audio of the water. From this, X. might have learned to be an outdoorsman. Instead, my first love acquired his love of electronics. His version of nostalgia was getting a VHS logo—in memory of the videos that had taught him to speak with no southern accent—tattooed on his arm. Or so I was told years after, a piece of information I record by inking it sentimentally on the page.

X. and I broke up decades ago and I don't keep in touch with my old friends. What I have stayed true to is my home, the mountains. When I speak of the landscape I love, people seem to think of Appalachian cul-ture isolated from outside influences, hidden in coves and hollows, a preserved, nobler, closer-to-the-land way of being. I doubt they picture scenes such as my memory of riding up steep roads going to a party with DJs held in a cave. Pill bottles rolling on the car floor marked the climbs and descents with their percussion. I was all sensation, feeling sounds as pleasure to my skin. It was no wholesome experience of nature, this leisure so unlike the labor of settling families who dug into their places by farming and with coal mining. But this was formative, and a part of those guitars and synthesizer, me as X.'s passenger, are what others must love if they love me now.

I learned of ballads from adaptations, weird spins on them by contem-porary musicians. After I finished high school and moved to the city, homesick, I'd ride with Will Oldham's voice as my companion: *Cow-call, and they were all calling together / Describing the way to go . . . / Withdraw, withdraw you live so far from town.* Missing X., I'd turn to Oldham singing, *If I could fuck a mountain, I would fuck a mountain,* so indelicately. Desire, of course, is impure, and ideas of chastity have always existed alongside dreams of breaking it.

My first love knew how to catch an Atlanta college station's signal if he parked at just the right angle outside our hometown Kmart. One evening, he mentioned the parking lot used to be his grandfather's apple orchard. That must have been the start, of wishing to go back to before I'd ever left, or the era before I existed, back to the earth below the pavement. Though I was also facing the road that had yet to carry my body to universities, where I'd learn and teach, to my husband and final love. Why is love, if measured by fidelity, supposed to mean never speaking of, seeming to show a capacity for utterly forgetting, earlier passions? A good refrain hooks you, a good ear remembers.

So I listen for the wind in the fruit trees, the bees. Sometimes the closest I can come to hearing them is in radio static, in traffic. I doubt I'll ever be in the range of X.'s voice again, though I think of him often. I try to keep in mind that the pollen that clings to bee's legs is the substance of another species' reproduction, nothing too clean. The bees, painted and flocked by flowers' extrusions, carry that potent gold home, faithful and humming.

ANOTHER INSCRUTABLE HOUSE

Dig into the hill
Dig into the hill's northside
Call your own name until
You have one
You have one
You have one

   —from "How to Build a Root Cellar," by Rebecca Gayle Howell

If none of this will be remembered, then let us keep speaking
with tongues light as screen doors clapping shut
on a child's finger. For this is love. To press
one frame against another

   —from "Someday I'll Love Roger Reeves," by Roger Reeves

1.

No language is available for the houses built in my lifetime and that, of late, I have spent my days among. They are not part of any one tradition, not true to a style through and through, cannot be understood, referred to with vocabulary such as Victorian or colonial or even revival of some kind.

I published a book of poems set in old houses, pure in their plainness and constant in their white paint, run round by farm fences, sited in the tight coves of the Southern Appalachian Mountains, where I'd lived my whole life. Then did what I thought a poet ought to do and began following teaching jobs across the country, away from home and between the towns tacked up around universities (their populations always graduating to the next class, taking down whatever posters they'd stuck with putty). My poetry did not progress. I would have liked to be a poet with the range of C. D. Wright, who, renowned for her southern voice as she was, declared, *I can only yammer and yam my way through so many hundreds of lines, living as I do between the Wisconsin Street Housing Project and the San Jose Freeway.* I would have liked to go on road trips and research projects in the manner of her wild books, which escape definition as either long poems or essays. But to get my bearings in the complexity of her work, I have to cling to the homey phrases such as *Peaches and fireworks and red ants. Now do you know where you are.* And though I have never been skilled with form or meter, after a couple of years adrift, I had begun confining my drafts to poor gestures toward such traditions, hammering sounds in, walling off the view of intended meaning for the sake of some stanzaic convention. Wandering through anonymous subdivisions, wordless, I thought of how, too freely, to contract and title and deed, I'd signed my name.

2.

Nameless as new constructions may be, in *House Without Names,* architectural historian Thomas Hubka argues we should still study, and thus acknowledge, the significance of the houses in which the majority of Americans now reside. And I must admit that even the historic architecture, the rustic relics, for which I get homesick—built without plans, by laymen, each of whom incorporated their own idiosyncrasies—didn't unvaryingly meet the criteria for saddlebag or dogtrot or shotgun houses. But there is language for those specimens that evolved as distinctly as their builders' accents in remote Appalachia: vernacular. *When we isolate from the world a neglected architectural variety and name it vernacular, we have prepared it for analysis,* writes Henry Glassie, scholar of folklore. *The term marks the transition from the unknown to the known.*

Rather than identifying facades and assigning buildings to categories as professionals have typically done to assess architecture, Hubka suggests any citizen can stand in the sidewalks gazing up and considering how a stranger's house, by those who possess its keys, is used. Even from outside, one can deduce that a chimney leads to an interior wall, the largest window signals the living room beyond, the smallest window the bath, and a window placed higher than the rest suggests a sink below—the kitchen. This isn't an admonition to be a peeping tom of the kind Ellen Bryant Voigt suspects of disturbing the sense of safety in her rural abode in *Headwaters: we heard it from our house where soon the shutters would go up / we sat in the kitchen the summer air soft as a damp rag we knew / this was a moment of consequence but we couldn't tell / whether the world had grown larger or smaller.*

But I did take Hubka's suggestion as a means of enlarging my perceptions, in the way Voigt, a poet famous for her *formal exactitude,* as she neared age seventy, abandoned punctuation and symmetry to *write a book of fresh beginnings.* And a spec house, if not distinguished much by appearance from the rest of the vinyl and laminate kits popped up in a row with it, became more interesting if I could guess that the explanation for the imbalanced number of doors is side access to the kitchen. That's where the lady of the house unloads groceries. Yes, there's the electric meter for confirmation—it runs to the room that appliances, as well as family and the most familiar friends, are fed in.

3.

Inscrutable is what I call my present house, which is little older than me. It looks like a basic child's drawing, a triangle topping a square. A brown homogenization of some Cape Cod, cabin, and modern gestures. An inarticulate rendering, I might say of it, as I have of my own writing, when none of it seemed worth fixing on the page.

The nickname is a reference to a poem: Elizabeth Bishop's "Sestina," her phrase, *the child draws another inscrutable house.* And vernacular houses, more venerated than mine, are hard to read too. They are houses for which no one has quite pinned down the qualities. Except that they are shaped by what the environment provides (the temperature and precipitation to be countered, the selection of wood or stone with which this may be done), plus what the builder can improvise. James Agee, in his 1941 classic *Let Us Now Praise Famous Men*, elucidates the beauty of houses constructed by the poor, with poor materials: *Most naïve, most massive symmetry and simpleness. Enough lines, enough off-true, that this symmetry is strongly yet most subtly sprained against its centers, into something more powerful than either full symmetry or deliberate breaking and balancing of "monotonies" can hope to be. A look of being most earnestly hand-made, as a child's drawing, a thing created out of need, love, patience, and strained skill.*

I suppose it is modernly vernacular that I bought the house I have, not because it is my or a designer's dream but because this is what I could find and could afford where I have work. But it's not just that I couldn't pay the mortgage for the few historic houses available in the vicinity of the university where I now teach. I did not want to occupy the legacy of the plantation mansions or turreted confections commissioned by the town-founding rich, subscribe to their aesthetics, not of shelter but of pure show of wealth. There must be some virtue in my house looking like a universal symbol, like it could belong to anyone.

4.

One structure with two front doors, two street numbers: these are the obvious exterior markers of a duplex. A house in which the interior wall is shared. The duplex is an architectural model that did originate—and was given a name—in this century.

The duplex is also a poetic form invented by Jericho Brown. It consists of seven couplets, with the last line of each stanza repeating in the first line of the next and the first word of the piece reappearing as the last but with a different resonance by the end. There is such timeless appeal to formal poems that reserve seats for envois and voltas, meet expectations of when the writer's name will be uttered, or deliver a reliable beat and the rhymes of one sound to answer another's call. It is from the legacies of sonnets, ghazels, and blues poems that the duplex is derived.

5.

Derived from, inspired by, an adaption of, a variation on a theme, with a similar ring: Do you hear such things? Do the influences show? Perhaps there are readers who will have already noted that this piece of mine is in seven couplets of prose and that each section's last word is the first word or few letters of the next. I doubt it though. My motif is not rendered with enough consistency or clarity (not like classical running patterns carved around Roman entrances, exits, and roofs). Nevertheless, there are elements that bear repeating. I made my own pattern with a *shuffling of erraticism, strictness yet subtle dishevelment*, to lift phrases about rough-hewn shingles composed by Agee, who considered himself a *thief* of the images of his subjects' houses. Or I borrowed some scaffolding permissive enough to let me raise my own *off-true* hybrid. There is also the appeal of *the mutt of a form as so many of us in this nation are only now empowered to live fully in all of our identities*—how Brown describes the duplex. There is the inspiration of something invented in this decade, by the young and living.

C. D. Wright is *part of a line of mavericks and contrarians who struggled to keep the language particular in times of ever-encroaching standardization*, in Ben Lerner's words. She, among the most *formally restless and ambitious writers of American English* to publish during my lifetime, is dead. But so freshly, it is a fact I am inclined to deny. Reading her inquiries, *What are you going to do when our lamps are out. / What are you going to do*, it seems she remains in active conversation with Agee, who preferred oil lamps to electrification and noted them all throughout *Let Us Now Praise Famous Men*. She carried on his torch as a southern documentarian who was aware she was an outsider spying on her subjects and as a genre bender too. In Agee's book (written late into many nights), he ends the section de-voted to the tenant farmers' kitchens he'd been studying with a depiction of a lamp out and casts it as lovely in that condition, like a young nude, in the dawning light of day. And he chose to devote a whole page to just two sentences, *The house had now descended / All over Alabama the lamps are out*, using white space for emphasis as in poetry. At the same time, *poetic* is also the effect of the densest parts of his rambling volume because he took a path counter to the convention of moving the narrative ahead. It is as if there is room and time for everything and we never have to leave. The text feels innovative even as it keeps readers hovering over the same curl of wood grain and the angle of each nail driven into the shack's frame, dwelling.

6.

Dwelling at my present address, over time, even if it is measured in contemporary hours, I am discovering layers. Beneath the understated brown paint, there are cedar boards, more expensive and more durable than the standard lumber, a little flourish the original owners allowed themselves in the 1970s. It must have been more recent still when they inserted the steel stove. I remind myself of how proud they must have been of its gleam when it strikes me as smudgy and anything but stainless and quite ostentatious in the small, beige kitchen. I will not venture, like Bishop, to the tropical setting of "Jeronimo's House." Will not take with me, through further relocations, the sights of his clapboard walls with *writing-paper lines of light* shining through the cracks and develop these into staggered little stanzas as she did. I have been granted tenure at the university where I work now. (Unlike real estate, with its monthly rents and evictions, *tenure,* when referring to an academic job, means permanence, no longer being subject to seasonal rehiring, a job at which I am permitted to keep laboring.) I will stay in this house and see it through its changes. I think of how I will add my own touch of beadboard over the popcorn ceiling someday and tell myself to stop trying to clean the fingerprints off appliances for the moment.

I've been filling my hours with reading in the front room. The previous occupants had furnished it as if it were a parlor from a bygone era in which nobody would ever be comfortable sitting. I've unpacked my books here and set up a library. They're alphabetized by name, as is usual—with exceptions for the volumes I need to keep closest at hand. (Among these is Voigt's earlier volume, *Kyrie*, a collection of sonnets about the 1918 influenza pandemic. In it, not worn out by summer as in the later poem I've already quoted, she writes about anticipating a spring that has yet to bring its warmth and hope and curtains open to receive them, *But it was true: at the window, / every afternoon, toward the horizon / a little more light before the darkness fell.*) I've gotten back to revising and writing. My terse early poems relied so on the voices of old-timers and locals already wise to whatever I wondered, implied meaning in brief lines' omissions. Now I'm doing research, discovering much information I want to include on the page. The lines grow longer each time I work on them again.

7.

Again and again, "Sestina" mentions its stove. It's defined by the dated detail of being *Marvel* brand. But then it undergoes transformation and becomes *marvelous* before the end. Maybe the sketching child grows up into a man who nails additions onto the house, and maybe these alter its historic character. Maybe that's okay because it means he's still following the winding path to and from that residence's door. Maybe he will renovate it with modern conveniences and replace the wood-burning stove. And it doesn't really matter because I don't think change to objects is the kind of change the aging woman cries over, though the specific reason for her tears isn't clear. What is almost certain is that readers of the poem share in the same resulting mourning feeling.

Also shared is the surety that the kitchen is where people will congregate. In the canonical past of the scene of "Sestina." Or in a future studio apartment with only an electric fry pan. In a farmhouse that kin go around back to enter, so as not to be a bother with their knocking. Or a McMansion (given only a pejorative name) in which the open floorplan offers any visitor a line of vision to the cook's mess, if not takeout cartons. In a house where you were reared. Or where I can only suppose what it is like to be welcomed over the threshold. Meals' ingredients may be stirred and seasoned by various members of a family or party as they lean on the counters and chat. And pieces of literature are social creations formed in response to and in concert with others as well. (See me crowding together many ideas into one paragraph trying to be like my model, the duplex.) When Wright wrote in "The Next to the Last Draft," *The author wanted / this book to be friendly, to say, Come up on the porch with / me, I've got peaches; I don't mind if you smoke,* I felt invited into the process. Now that I have chased writing so far, I hear Wright's echo in remote streets: *She will still be up when we come in. Our floating host. She will be at the door in her pleated nightgown. Admit us into her air-conditioned nightgown. Her glory cloud.* The kitchen's lights are first to turn on in the morning and last illuminated in the dark. The kitchen's glow can help a walker, pausing to gather herself so she can keep moving, as she imagines her way to the heart of the home, that place we all do know.

SETTLING IN

1. The Surroundings (Only Stone)

The region offers no mineral wealth except stone and has *scenic beauty but little else,* a government official wrote of Pine Mountain, where my husband and I chose to move. What more could we need? Of the beauty, a park has been made.

A park with humble features that lay low. It was constructed during the Great Depression by the Civilian Conservation Corps, and the Forest Service's "Acceptable Building Plans" from that time state that buildings *seldom enhance the beauty of their natural settings.* So, these constructions counter the style of resorts before (which had risen with a fussy show of Victorian decoration) and after (now aspiring high with slick steel and glass impositions).

The horizontal designs of the park buildings do not try to compete with the lines and loft of trees. The stone walls are assembled from live-edged slabs hewn only as square as necessary for stacking and no farther away from the original shape geology made.

The park is named for Franklin Delano Roosevelt, who came here to sink into the warm springs and try to cure his paralysis from polio. In that, he did not succeed. But he loved the area and made it the site of his Little White House, 130 rooms fewer than the official presidential residence. Also the place where he died.

A statute was erected in his memory. Or rather—unlike the statues of leaders that usually show them standing proudly or as floating heads of forever chin-up busts—a figure of FDR is seated on the mountain.

The most sizable of the Depression-era work projects undertaken in the vicinity is a negative space—a ten-acre lake excavated by hand. How many men reduced to going on relief worked themselves below the surface to achieve this hole?

It must have been arduous, shoveling through quartzite, an especially hard stone that studs the local earth. But we're dug in here. My love and I will stay.

And quartzite *is* a resource. It is good material for the foundations of homes. Because quartzite lasts longer than granite, it's good for grave markers as well.

2. Master Bath (Ambitious Plans)

The house is set so unobtrusively in the landscape that we need no lawn mower and so deeply that the bathroom requires no curtains. The brown exterior paint blends in. The scale is modest. Except for master bathroom, which occupies presumptuously much space. It puzzled us, how the standards of our predecessors, in this bathroom, slipped. Until we considered they were elderly, and the bars and handles mounted in the tile all around.

They must have had the hope that if they were able to roll, seated, into the shower—big enough for a wheelchair—they could stay. Had the ambition to continue just as they were, to live away from people, surrounded by, beneath a heavy canopy of, leaves.

That ambition, of course, had to fail; that's why we could move into their place. The couple learned. As we—stooping to the level of the handrails and looking out to the view of trees, what are desirable to see—are beginning to learn. About growing closer to the earth and being lowered down into it then.

3. The Garden Statuary (I Carried Them Briefly)

I drove the statues to the town where we used to live, put the whole collection of cement cherubim and puppy-clutching plastic children on the curb. In a place where they might be wanted. We moved into the woods to be far from other people and could not abide the garden decor, clutter the earlier owners left under foot.

Even the girl figurine, who was revealed to be plastic when her head broke open somewhere along the miles of winding road, would be claimed by morning. I told myself this, back at my new home, as I tried to sleep. I thought of her and of when, on garbage day, our old neighbors displayed, in piles separate from trash, items that could get another generation of use. Car seats, football helmets, wings for extending dining tables, inflatable pools—these things would be taken and had a future with other families.

At our current place, I have not gotten rid of the little artificial water feature installed next to my office door, though I stopped chlorinating and tinting it an unnatural blue. I caught mosquito fish from the stream on the property to eat the larvae gathering in the water. Now the mosquito fish are *gravid*—the word usually used to describe species of the non-mammal classes and their pregnancies. But while most fish lay eggs, mosquito fish give live birth, like my own breed.

On the pool's side is the one statue I kept because it is fixed to a fountain that burbles from between his feet, aerating the fish's water. (Now I could not do without the sight of his small human form.) When the mothers release their young, I know I will kneel close beside this chubby fellow, this cupid—or a baby of some kind—to watch as the bodies multiply.

4. The Arbor (After Moving, Trying to Get Old Friends to Make the Long Drive)

We have an arbor covered in Carolina jessamine. Not Confederate jasmine, another vine with which some have confused it. This arc is what friends will walk through when they take their first steps out of the car. It's an arbor that's a trellis. We have let the bearer of yellow trumpet flowers overgrow it to be welcoming.

Our gardening book describes the plant as *well-mannered, climbs beautifully without smothering the surrounding shrubs.* These blossoms are of no relation to the Confederate monument in the town square, a sore loser sulking, *Fate denied them victory.* Just because we live here now doesn't mean we claim that history. (The origin of the name jessamine, by the way, is Persian.)

The jessamine scales to the tops of trees, blooms well before they have leaves. The plant is not what you might think, seeing it crowning everything—it's not an invasive species. And it wins every spring.

5. The Boundaries (Spring Is in the Air Again)

The burn was controlled. So, though we could see its alarming amber and red through our trees and smoke settled on our little plot, we were told not to worry. The neighbor told us that the fire would not cross property lines, was set intentionally. It was to clear out the undergrowth attempting to mix into his pine plantings, his three hundred acres of precisely spaced, unvarying species. This was last spring.

We should not worry. After all, the neighbor is the fire chief. The neighbor who lives to the right of us, that is.

Rumor has it that the other adjoining property owner—to our left—had a problem in the past with flames overreaching, and the fire chief took his burn permit away. We have yet to meet the left-hand neighbor. We have not seen him out working in his eventual timber, where vines snarl in the rows.

We have recently learned that the men on either side of us are brothers.

We hear the locals still puzzling, decades after, over how their father could have divided the family land equally among the two, with no regard for waywardness or merit. We hear speculation about how the fire chief will have to relent and allow something to be done before that undergrowth next door becomes a danger, as kindling and fuel itself. And people still wonder about the feelings between the brothers. Do they still rage? How long can kin keep apart?

We are still waiting for someone to mention our little parcel, to explain how it has come to be between the two halves of the old plantation. The air, however, is not still. Burning season is approaching.

6. The Bedroom (Arising)

A bulge is pressed up from below the surface of the garden soil. Then some mottled purplish flesh shows. It's the tip of the shaft that elongates, grows every day. It reaches several feet in length, begins to drip, and thickens. Until it bursts open.

Then it releases, not some sensual culmination but the smell of rot. It is a carrion flower. What rises now conjures thoughts of flesh's demise. The prior resident of what is now our house, a horticulturist and the wife of a minister, is responsible for the contents of this garden. She tended all of it—the flowers, the trees grown to maturity, the shrubs now tall enough to cast shade—for forty years. Yet she could not protect her husband from growing old and ill.

While we strive to maintain the landscape in the condition in which we received it, we are renovating the room where we sleep. As the construction workers demolish a wall, the pack begins to howl. Men—I am reminded that my husband, deep cleaning the shower grout beside me, is one of them.

Stuffed behind the drywall the men had found rolled pages now spilling free with a great unfurling of nipple, navel, and thigh. *Playboys.*

Calculating what I know of the prior residents and dates and factoring in a few baseball cards mixed with the magazines, I figure when the minister's son would have been a teenager. This must have been his room. He must have hidden these pages from his chastening parents' view.

Though who am I to make assumptions about the couple, when the lady of the house set the plants that awaken surprise in us daily. She chose the varieties to ensure something would be blooming in every season of the year. And don't my love and I want to be here until we die, spend decades more in the house and with each other's bodies?

I want the workmen to clear out of our quarters, leave us in privacy. I do not wish we had chosen a different master bedroom. Our days have a youthful point of beginning: Mornings we rise where the studs held, to later disclose, this lusty show.

7. The Paths (Laid, Please, So as Not to Lead Away)

My husband has laid paths across every bend and turn of our property. With rake and hoe, scythe and handsaw—all with his hands. (Often without his shirt, I can't help adding, though there's nothing more than descriptive words I'd be willing to share of him.) He's laid paths to the triple-trunked sycamore with the shape intended for our swing hanging beneath. To the rocks splayed by the stream, offering a place for picnic dinners. To the hilltop overlook from which we can gaze. Down the bank, digging stairs into the dirt to guide my steps to the cave we call *secret,* so slender that it presses two adults into intimacy. And through the laurel, designating a route (though we must bend double to fit through the snarl of trunks) for observing the dam and how beavers work to strengthen what is theirs.

Soon, I laugh, his trail making will turn to spiraling, given the limits of our acreage. I also have the sense to insist that one patch of woods remain with its floor undisturbed. Our little unmapped territory. Intently, I've watched my lover, sweating. But when he approaches where I've been observing, I move away from the window or pull the curtain, as if to change my dress. Or when he returns from his labor, I am behind the bathroom door, deep under perfumed bathwater. I want there to be somewhere left for him to go, so the day does not come when he thinks these property lines are constraints his passion cannot keep within.

8. The Roof (Over Our Heads)

Our new roof is supposed to last forty years. Plantation pines are cut on a forty-year rotation. This means that at the time the roof fails, the hundreds and hundreds of acres of trees that surround us will be cleared.

The previous owners lived in this house for forty years, then—after falling became a risk for one—sold. Will we still be standing when this new green metal we're buying to raise above us wears through?

I am over forty myself—so old, I thought as a kid, that if life didn't end by now, it would certainly be sagging in death's direction. At least my breasts so far suggest otherwise. And the expensive roof, meant to shelter us in an interior kept separate from the outside world, is the color of fresh, free-growing leaves.

We'll do what needs to be done about the house when it's time to. The idea behind a farm for lumber is that the trees regrow. The idea behind the bills of sale we've cosigned is that, together, the lovers go.

9. The Gate (Symbolism)

Though I'd spent years opposed to gates, I didn't get rid of the one on the property we bought. I'd thought of gates as erected by people who had the money for second homes, which they built on top of the Blue Ridge Mountains I am from. Gates were to keep locals—who had grown up in and knew faithfully that place—at a distance from the rich's *getaways* from their other lives.

The previous owner of our property told me the story of our gate, which began with him purchasing two stone pineapple finials at an estate sale. (Price-tagged and laid out on a table: This is how some inheritances are conveyed.) After he had the antiques, he felt he ought to supply columns on which they could reside. And once those were constructed by a stonemason, it began to seem something ought to span the space between. He ordered a gate, with an electric keypad, into which a code must be pressed, so a hydraulic arm swings it open.

The pineapple is supposed to be a symbol of hospitality. When the fruits were first imported to Europe from overseas, they were so expensive and rare that to have one at your party was to demonstrate tremendous care for your guests. Pineapples were so valued that they were displayed until they shriveled, rather than eaten for one's own pleasure.

Of course, from a more global and practical perspective, the pineapple is a symbol of colonialism. Columbus, or some other exploiter, discovered the exotic delicacy. He created the export demand that, today, Third World workers bend over fields of spiny plants to supply, while pesticides run off and pollute their water. In the United States, in the South in particular, many a maid with a pineapple stitched on her uniform's breast piles pineapple-studded fruit salads in breakfast buffets that cost twice her hourly minimum wage. It is really wealth and power that pineapples, like gates, illustrate.

But though I am a newcomer to this area, my mind tends toward the local and small. Poems are what I know, and I recall these lines by Bin Ramke,

What makes a garden is a gate. What makes a gate is a fence—otherwise it is a trellis.

While the pineapple has a thick-skinned, barbed exterior, the iron gate the previous owner chose is not so forbidding. Each point is tipped with a pineapple shape. And only a body as large as a car needs the code, to go through the gate, to access the property. There is no fence, just acres of open land fanning out from either column. Around the sides scamper the neighborhood kids, toward the creek, as their grandparents did. Every hot day, I can hear their shrieks of pleasure at the rapids, as they let themselves be swept away.

I hope the reverend is happy to see his gate standing when his nurse or grown child drives him by. *Reverend*—I ought to refer to him as true community members do. He was a minister, I should remember.

Today the gate's electric keypad was smote by lightning. I'll pay to have it replaced, pay to keep the gate, in honor of the earthly things he let himself care for.

10. The Amphitheater (Filling the Hole)

We call it the amphitheater. A sudden semicircle where the earth drops off for twenty or more feet, a shock when we first happened upon it, walking through our woods. It is an old excavation, perhaps from road construction.

The road—the paved, public one well beyond sight from the house—is officially a *street*. It was designated as such by planners in a past century, who imagined progress of a kind that has not come. We are glad greater numbers of people have not been inserted among the county's population of trees. Though old friends, in the messages they send or on the rare occasion we see them since we've moved out to this land, ask where we shop, what we'd do for work if we couldn't commute, about the travel time to the hospital. The answer to the latter is that we'd have to drive this road, then another, and another for a long time.

The crater's, the amphitheater's, sides are so sheer that there are spots where the red clay still shows. Though the road this earth may have been taken to build is old enough that the pavement is now cracking. And vegetation is gradually rooting in the amphitheater. We don't do any clearing, install seating, or dress up a thing. We do not act at all. Let trout lilies cling in uncut bouquets and laurels bestow their own boughs on the hole. Let them fill the roles. We live here. We determined that, and now our lives will play themselves out.

11. The Rock Walls (Always Stones)

Some people throw stones at others. Some people weight their own pockets with stone and wade into the lake.

Some people I've known skipped the thinnest stones over the surface of the water to the far shore. Some I remember seeing slip a smooth stone into their pocket to soothe them wherever they were going to go.

One gathers substantial stones on long walks and packs them home on his back.

Most people, says the guidebook to stone masonry, will first pick up a stone too large for the hole to be filled. Also that most people will think they've collected enough stones for their project before they have half of what they need.

It will take my love years and years of carrying rocks out of the forest to collect as much rock as he could pay to have a dump truck deposit in a day.

He fits all the odd little rubble, the pieces of local quartzite, despite their not being even or level, together to build a sturdy wall.

Each anniversary, I give him a rock tied in satin ribbon. The project and these presents being his wish: I do not want him to ever finish.

VESSELS

If land is to be left, it determines by what means. Where there were cedars, cedars were carved into floating shapes that bore people into the water. Where there were birches, birch bark was curved into canoes. The arctic, lacking trees, was the site of the kayak's invention, humans stretching terrestrial animals' skins around frames of bone. Whatever did grow was turned into the boat of the locale.

Crafts particular to their regions kept developing. The pirogue used in Louisiana bayous is of the cypresses rooted in their soil, soil barely covered by the water the shallow boat is suited to be poled through. The marshy stretches of the northern Atlantic inspired the Ducker (of Delaware) and Sneakbox (of New Jersey), while high-sided dories and dinghies originated in response to the region's high seas. On the far coast, Oregon's McKenzie and Rogue Rivers each have a boat particular to the currents and breakers of their fresh waters.

In Southern Appalachia, the Cherokee made their dugouts by felling trees so great they had to be burned and hollowed right where they lay before they were light enough to budge. The Cherokees' land was seized, and after, in the hands of this region's settlers, no distinctive prow or paddle or hull, no particular modern boat, evolved. This is the area where I am from (though not *native* to), where the heritage of centuries of removal is maybe fittingly reflected by absence of a contemporary endemic boat.

When my father wanted to float the river that flows through the mountains we consider home, he had to choose a boat from elsewhere in America. Our mountains are worn low by time, and the river takes time, moves slow. So my father settled on the Ozarkian johnboat. The johnboat became the only kind he would own. Its prow is unpointed, its bed flat. It is not shaped to travel with any speed, to respond to steering readily. But the vessel is steady, and I remember him standing in it to cast, out on the water, as if the earth were still beneath his feet.

The johnboat goes by the first name commonest among men. Nobody presumes to christen one of these boats with the allusions to pretty ladies inscribed on fancier starboards and portsides. But what does a name matter? For a human, it is a gift given early that, traditionally, no matter the fit, they will not exchange. The johnboat became the tradition of which I am inheritor. A tradition a single generation old but all I can claim to know.

Tracks of aluminum, from where our boat scraped to a stop on snags, trailed behind us. Protestations laid on the stone, scrawls of metal. Or shimmering inscriptions, silver lines of cursive, I'd like to call them. I'd like to say our story, short and written in water, made a gesture to counter all those exalting forward trajectories, being conveyed to another world or taking a new one. As if we could go back.

NO DUMMY

Fork-tender, a hyphenate, is the phrase for the delicacy I wanted to achieve for the stringy turkey before putting it on a plate. This was meat my husband shot, this was early, before I could claim him with that name. The bird is one of the first offerings he ever brought me.

Tower kill refers to when birds fly into cell towers and, from the impact, die. The existence of this term means a great many have, in this manner, ceased to be. Birds have stopped singing because of how we've sent out our calls.

Yet I've kept on with words. When my love took up pursuit of different game, fishing, I learned that a fly tier bringing together feathers to make a lure describes the action as *marrying.* Also, those who are less lofty than anglers and baitfish instead may dangle maggots from their hooks, referring to them colloquially as *gentles.*

And I've read that the scales of little fish who bore the name of *bleaks* were nevertheless used in the manufacture of artificial pearls. *Artificial* or *costume* or *faux.*

My love is none of these, though I can't be sure how well I've ever managed to tell feelings to him.

I do know there's a word for the enormous perfume bottles displayed above cosmetic counters: *factice.* Better that than *dummy.* I know those models hold only colored water. But I can ask the salespeople for samples, get little vials of the real thing, and the vessel, at that scale, is full.

Small fry are little fish. *Hard fry* is to cook fish crispy, through and through.

To play *hardball* is to be unyielding. *Hardball* is also the stage when the sugar is hot enough that it is time for the candy to be formed, when syrup clings to the spoon, ropy and sweetly binding.

Yield can refer to ceasing to argue, to texture that lets touch sink in, or how much a recipe or a tended field gives to feed us at the end. I was speaking of tenderness when, with piercing tines, I chose to begin.

WITHOUT CONCLUSION

The Cherokee word for *black snake* translates to *one who is climbing continuously*. Or this is what I understand from what I've read.

I like the idea of continuousness, how it modifies the meaning of the movement away and how many English words can be expressed jointly in a lithe one of the language Tsalagi.

▲

The link I have to this information comes from my mother, her daily email passing on an article from my hometown newspaper. I have no Cherokee heredity. All that connects me to the culture is proximity.

I grew up near what was the tribe's principal settlement, Cowee, in present-day Macon County, North Carolina. In the adjoining county is Cherokee, tribal property, which tourists might know only as the site of a casino, golf course, petting zoo, and shops offering tomahawks.

▲

In the 1970s, Werner Herzog came to Cherokee to film the conclusion of *Stroszek*. In the movie, a German immigrant, Bruno, travels across the country losing his money, his home, and all the people he loves as he goes. I am a fan of the film, flattered that Herzog could have gone anywhere in the world and chose to come to the region I know best, even if it was to capture the culmination of many failings.

No matter the context, when I hear the word *Cherokee*, I thrill a little at the link to familiar geography. *Nantahala, Cullowhee*, when I encounter them referenced on any page, conjure warm thoughts of the town with a bookstore I had steered my Ford Escort toward as a teenager and of the deep forest and river where my mother took me to walk and swim when I was small.

I attended Iotla and Cowee Elementaries. At the doors of a school with a Cherokee name, I learned my first lesson about loss, having to walk away from my mother, that first day of class. The loss was so minor, though in my naïveté, it felt like tragedy. She instructed me that I did not need the help of the little boy who offered to carry the backpack hanging to my knees and then began to weep at our separation.

I know now, of course, of Bureau of Indian Affairs boarding schools intended to unteach Native children their culture. Schools took thousands from their families forever, forced them to cut their hair and wear European clothes, convert to Christianity, and speak English alone. I've read the accounts of children's mouths being scrubbed out if they were heard uttering words of the language that was their own, and worse punishments and tortures.

Now Cowee, the small, rural school, closed for a decade, has reopened as a community center, with my mother on the board of directors. In the room where I struggled over long division, there are plans to open a museum of the Cherokee.

The signage at Cowee School was recently reprinted in the syllabary. After the first new signs were hung, a speaker of Tsalagi informed the center's board members that the sign intended to say *Cowee* actually read *home,* specific to no geography.

▲

I would like to believe I could find home again, away from acres demarcated by the climbing roses my mother planted to drape her barbed wire fences. But I have moved around the country and encountered no other place like it, no such comfort.

The denouement of *Stroszek* is a montage. There's a scene of the protagonist's, Bruno's, truck—afire—circling amid a souvenir shop teepee and a Cherokee street performer wearing a Plains Indian's feathered headdress. Meanwhile, Bruno rides a ski lift up the mountain, presumably to shoot himself. The picture cuts back and forth between these scenes and close-ups of a caged chicken that dances when money is inserted in a machine. I interpret this as a story of the falsity of the American Dream, of how we will all be defeated by capitalism in this nation that, at its inception, tried to ruin the Native people.

▲

I can read Herzog's symbols, but I cannot read the characters of the Cherokee syllabary, cannot understand any of the language that is original to my home.

Chero-honky is a neologism I've recently heard. The slang that Black speakers coined to refer to a Caucasian person has been compounded into a new term for white people who appropriate and imitate.

▲

I will admit I keep thinking of how Cherokee society is matrilineal and of the thread connecting me to my mother, how it is the most supreme binding I have.

In the 1500s, Native people cleared fields such as the one by the river where my mother grew timothy grass. Where she stacked hay bales into playhouse walls, spreading my grandmother's quilt over the top, one more layer of shelter.

▲

When I imagine the fields, as my mother gets older, no longer seeded and cut, that cycle unmaintained—being lost to weeds—there is nothing that can stop my eyes from flooding.

In a lecture, a teacher of poetry said that sometimes the topics people are drawn to write about may be like reflexive pain. Meaning that, though a pain may be felt in your shoulder, the pulled muscle in your calf could be the source. That if you think you want to write about a major cultural injustice, it may be because you actually want to write about some smaller suffering of your own.

▲

Of course, there are people whose history precedes anything I could have ever thought was mine.

Of course, there are people whose losses far exceed any I will know.

▲

Can there be art that comes of reflective admiration? How to relate a story or feeling without seeming to lay claim? How to express empathy or wonder without seeming to equate others' experiences to my own?

▲

One of the first phrases I spoke as a child was *Mommy shovel, Daddy type.* I was explaining the structures of our family's particular little culture.

I have turned out to be the typing sort, a writer who only exerts herself trying to manage words. Though my earliest speech was about my mother's power, recognizing her strength was not the same as asserting likeness between us.

▲

There are only about two hundred speakers of North Carolina's Eastern dialect of Cherokee and most are over age fifty today.

But Tsalagi is not a dead language. More young people are studying it with the elders.

▲

Tsalagi is one of the most challenging languages to learn, a teacher acknowledges in the newspaper article.

A language cannot be saved by singing a few songs or having a word printed on a postage stamp (or poster). It cannot even be saved by getting "official status" for it, or getting it taught in schools. It is saved by its use (no matter how imperfect), someone posts in the comments section of article about learning Cherokee.

▲

Native folklore, I have read, should not be expected to provide a pairing of every single thing with a secondary meaning. There may not be a precise metaphor or clear lesson to extract, as there are from parables in the European tradition delivering their grand finales.

▲

I want to say something about my mother's influence, how she carries on in the actions of this person she shaped. What poetic image could I join to such pure statement to make it more literary?

The laurel branches my mother gathered from our woods at Halloween and stitched to my bear-shaped backpack for a tree costume—were these to illustrate to me being authentically rooted and a creature ascending?

▲

I picture mother's hands painting sections of my hair with bleach, followed by red dye, washing and tinfoil wrapping and waiting at each stage. Was the waiting an analogy for my maturing? Were the streaks that she lamented looked like blood (but granted me anyway because I was a teenager and that was my desire) representations of the harm of the larger world from which she could no longer provide protection? Or was her creating them, making a mark on my head that I couldn't have achieved without her help, a reminder of our blood, our genes, in common, even as I outwardly changed?

No few moments are sufficient to define the love she put into my living. But these are better than nothing. And even if I could capture and record every action of hers, I wouldn't be content with just her one lifespan, to let it end. It is a blessing that there are histories, memories, links, greater than ours.

▲

A mother is a leader who wants her young to clamber after her as best they can, to survive their ignorance as she survives her own wearing down.

It takes students years to learn Tsalagi. Some must be puzzled to find that it does not have equivalents for all the words of English. To find that instead of *goodbye*, it is necessary to use a more complex phrase such as *let us see each other again.*

▲

While the Cherokee language often forges many connections in one word, it does make a distinction between words for animate and inanimate things. The language varies the way colors are applied to each. So there is one way of speaking of the color gray if applied to a stone. And, I'm guessing, hoping, it wouldn't be the same as the word used to describe the shade that the hair on a living woman's head turns.

Black, as in the color of a mourner's dress, must be distinguished from the black of a bear who has been hibernating (perhaps with cubs she's been nursing for months, grown hungry). Who will bring her body back up out of the earth, show her sun-reflecting fur—

WHAT I COULD TEACH A CHILD

In winter, if you lie low on the ground, the way animals do, you can slip beneath the cold examinations of the wind.

In the market, standing at the okra bin, sorting, it does not really matter whether you pinch the middle of the pod like some of the women or bend the tip like others. Some will make gumbo, some curry, and you'll be there, up to the wrist with all of them.

I'll pass on no recipes, but we'll make stew after stock out of whatever is in the bottom of the jar, the back of the cupboard. Our tastes and fingers in the pot are what will determine if a note is missing.

Be local and understand the speech of the handyman, that when he calls and says, *My truck is tore up,* he means that his vehicle isn't functioning and that he isn't coming to help with the plumbing.

There is no need for him; the well can be unfrozen with a hair dryer.

Air-dry your hair. It will stay shinier. Wash it the night before. In the morning, wear it as if effortless.

Be down to earth and use words economically. Cultivate the powers of double meaning and metaphor. Also, alliterate lavishly, let the music be great, a marvel that swells.

See the vastness of the ocean young.

Hear, along with the sound of the waves, the sound of restaurant staff closing up, and hear that china and silver clink as soothing too because it sounds like home. It sounds like my mother putting a kettle on the stove in the morning. Listen to find what will be your bell, when you need it, to ring familiar.

But be the kind who wades into the freshening sea, doesn't just sit in the resort's heated pool with a view. If there are no jellyfish and the water is going out. (We'll scan for tentacles, read the tide tables.)

On our property, watch the branches the fallen but still living oaks send up; these branches grow tall, no matter the low horizon lines of their trunks. Understand that gnarls form when trees pick up rocks in their roots and later release them, leaving smooth openings in their rough bark. They don't have to be illustrations of any moral, though.

Or consider that the knotholes may be doors for fairies (though you probably should not admit, after a certain age, that you think about them). Even the silliest imaginings must have hiding spots and homes.

To catch a kitten under a bush or in a ditch or a goat escaped from the pen, don't stand, shadow casting, don't be quick moving. Approach hunkered and from the side and never grab and seize. Extend your hand gently until you can encircle what you don't presume belongs to you but that may be happy in your hold.

RAILWAY COUPLING

A big top tent is forever pitched in the cemetery where I walk today—one carved from marble to memorialize a 1915 crash of a train carrying a circus. The stone says *Erected by The Con T. Kennedy Shows.* But Con T. Kennedy, owner, didn't die here in Columbus, Georgia. The Columbus newspaper says performers, *a caravan of misfits,* including dwarfs and Siamese twins and carloads of animals, did—by fire.

I'd been reading about orphan trains. In the mid-1800s through the 1920s, orphan trains relocated hundreds of thousands of children from eastern cities, many of whom had been living on the streets, westward to rural communities. These carloads of urban kids were adopted by farming families. I live in the country; Columbus is the nearest city. Where my online searching has taken me is to this rock, this local curiosity.

▲

The names of the circus dead aren't listed, a writer for *Roadside America* supposes, because *the mixed-up ashes of the train, animals, and people were shoveled here* together. There was no means of assessing differences in bodies—fur or feathers, scales or skin, air- or waterborne, bipedal or on all fours, the opposability or not of their toes. These distinctions were broken down by fire and burial.

I've been trying to adopt a baby. She will not be an orphan. She will be a joy to me. Yet somehow I've wound up thinking about her beside a mass grave, like a war atrocity. This is no place to make a case for the blurring of identities and genealogies.

▲

There is no situation resulting in a child's adoption that has been what the birth mother wanted. She may not have been allowed to make decisions about her own body, probably has not had access to just health care or social services that would enable her to choose to keep her baby.

The situation of the cemetery bears no metaphorical relation to a birth mother of an adopted child and her complexly deathless loss. Perhaps I've chosen, without admitting it before, to frequent cemeteries because they provide a setting for feeling sorry for myself, feeling my life is passing as I wait.

▲

The one choice a mother placing her infant for adoption is finally given, by agencies like the one I am working through, is to select the adoptive parents. She is given booklets of would-be mommies' and daddies' profiles, flips through page after page of formulaic answers to questionnaires about our careers and our favorite holidays and picture after picture of faces that are mostly white, like mine.

For four years, my profile has not been the one any birth mother has chosen from the stacks. This is why I take long walks, down train tracks, through any public space where I am allowed to wander. On the surfaces of the graves, all the faux flowers fade to a similar pallor.

▲

Fred Kempf was one of the better-known victims of the train crash, one of the few identified, a white man. His remains were stored in a vault in Georgia until family members could collect and take them back north to Michigan. I've read more about his family than any others associated with the tragedy, but they didn't want him to stay; his bones are elsewhere.

There are many reasons an expectant woman considering adoption might not want to send a child to my rural Georgia address. It's the state of the cotton gin's invention, of plantations and ports where humans were shipped in to be enslaved, the region second only to the Mississippi Delta for lynchings following the Civil War, where Ahmaud Arbery was lynched in 2020.

Kempf was famous for building the Kempf Model City, a miniature rendered in tremendous detail, powered by sewing machine motors. There was a lake with drawbridges that went up and down. Figures waved from houses' interiors. In the theater, there was a performance with trapezes and five scene changes. Lights clicked on in the factory for the night shift, and individually sculpted bananas lay in the fruit stand, promising morning and another day of these patterns. At the mill, according to *Popular Electricity*, 1911, men carried lumber into sheds and *returned empty handed*. I assume they then circled to lift their next load and their hands were full again. Every three minutes, the church bells rang.

My childhood memories are of building stick and leaf houses and doors for fairies in the gnarls of trees while my mother worked in the orchard. Of wearing dresses she made that matched my dolls'. I want to repeat such pleasures with another little girl.

Among the most remarkable constructions of the early 1900s, Kempf's model was called. It was a novelty the world wanted to see. So, after devoting his teenage years to working on the city, intent on his goal of precisely reproducing his homeplace, he took his creation and his own young family on the road. He outfitted an automobile like a house for them and parked it on the flatbed, its wheels stilled. The flatbed was coupled to the other cars in the train but, in many senses, separate from the rest of the circus party.

Among the children currently available for adoption, Caucasians are the rarity. I have not specified that I want a child of the same race as me. So, likely, my daughter will not look like me; it will be harder to find a doll that matches her in color; she will never experience entering gatherings, moving through spaces, with the safety and ease I have.

▲

In the accident, Kempf, his wife, and daughter were penned in the immovable automobile. The parents managed to pass the child out of the crushed vehicle, stretching their arms only so far as the shoulders and as would convey her to others' hands. Before the blaze got them.

The orphan trains were, arguably, more humane than the preceding complete lack of help for needy minors. Yet many of the passengers were not orphans at all. A child might have been urged on board without being told where she was going while her parent was in jail or the hospital. Or a mother, alive and well, might have signed away custody of a child because she could not feed him.

▲

Kempf's brother came to collect, along with the physical traces of Fred, the child, Hazel. Hazel Kempf would live comfortably off a settlement from the railroad company and the payment from the insurance for the model city. In Michigan, she'd have a house, a pony. Wouldn't her mother have been pleased by the life her daughter was handed into?

Other famous Georgia orphans (or *orphans* are what they were called) I've come across in my online wandering are the Hicks babies, whose stories began in the 1960s. They were infants delivered by Dr. Hicks, a doctor offering medical services to impoverished women, and then sold to wealthier families for as much as a thousand dollars. An infertile couple who desperately wanted a child recounts driving from Ohio and having a still bloody baby passed through the car window to them in the dark.

Today a mother who has placed her infant for adoption must be discharged from the hospital, perhaps to walk past pastel balloons or bouquets that have been brought for the new adoptive parents, her breasts tight with milk, abdomen and arms empty. Her eyes, I imagine, whether they hold back or overflow with tears, aren't likely to fill the sense of absence or release all her grief.

That the Kempfs were able to save their living miniature, if not their own human forms, does not make their conclusion sweet.

Prof A. U. Eslick's twenty-seven-piece brass band had burned in the circus train wreck. So locals loaned survivors instruments to play at the funeral of their coworkers (or their lovers, brothers, mothers). Newspaper headlines of the time, and stories to come later in nostalgic feature sections, reported on how Columbus's citizenry rallied to support the mourners. But *loaned* implies to be given back, and who owns what pieces of property is often remembered better than the dead.

Many of the children adopted from orphan trains in the 1800s were expected to pay back their adopters with labor, to earn their keep. Some were treated like indentured servants, abused. And there are plenty of contemporary narratives about adopted children made to feel that they must display gratitude for every bit of parenting they receive.

Really, the story of the train crash is about class. *Victims All Show People,* a newspaper headline assured. It was a car stuffed full of the poor that was destroyed. A train with costly seats, speeding ahead of schedule, struck the on-time circus performers'. Not a single person on the train of richer passengers was injured.

Sometimes Dr. Hicks told women whose babies he delivered that the newborns had died, when really they were healthy and to be sold. Perhaps he justified this deception as means to fund the abortions and other health services he provided for those who could not pay, though it's hard to apply the word *care* to any part of what he did.

Due to the transient nature of show people, the exact number killed in the circus accident and buried in Columbus was never determined. They were let go by history.

The mothers of children put on the orphan trains had to sign paperwork, including phrases such as *I hereby promise not to interfere.* Dr. Hicks kept no records of who the birth mothers of the infants he sold were, issued fake birth certificates under the purchasers' names. For decades, adoptions were closed—birth mothers were supposed to turn over their kids and disappear, records were sealed, and children were never told anything about the people whose bodies made them. These practices were said to protect the women's honor and privacy.

▲

Yes, Columbus's residents helped with the burial for crash victims. But their anonymity reveals that this was not an act of honoring humanity. There were corpses, and relatives could not be called to collect them. Burial was a necessity.

I have promised that someday—after all the waiting and rejection and paperwork and court dates are over and an adoption is finalized—I will keep interacting with the birth mother, if she wishes. I am to speak of her to my daughter regularly. The birth mother may ask that I send letters and pictures to her and set up visits. My social worker invites her children's various biological family members for Christmas every year. To be honest, when she tells me this, I feel frightened. Nevertheless, when she suggests hanging my daughter's birth mother's photo in our home, because it seems I ought to, I say *yes*.

▲

In the adoption application process, I have been examined physically, emotionally, financially, in nearly every way. I have had my house inspected (especially the smoke alarm and fire extinguisher) and provided letters of reference, birth and marriage certificates, hundreds of pages of documentation.

About Hazel's mother, I know little. She is referred to as Myrtle in one source and Blanche in others.

▲

The birth mother can also choose not to interact or to disclose personal information, and in that case, I will know almost nothing about her. I won't know, with certainty, about the history relevant to my child's health. Did the birth mother choose to check the boxes on forms that would tell me about the cancer running all through her family? Does anyone know if the biological father had diabetes, hypertension, depression? I won't be sure of the risks and deaths my daughter's genes make more likely. Fates that, as a mother, I am supposed to envision so as to fight to deter.

The immolated Blanche, if that was her name, could be identified only by the jewelry she had worn—a necklace in the cinders.

▲

At first, I thought I feared open adoption for my daughter's sake, was worried about how she might be hurt if the birth mother was unstable. But over time, I came to admit that what scared me was the chance that if they met and got along too well, my daughter would prefer the real mother—who I am not.

At least, in the context of an adoption application, many of the negative answers that I provide reflect on my candidacy favorably. I tested negative for diseases, negative for drugs. My fingerprints have been cleared from association with any criminal record by the state and feds. I have never been to court. I have never been divorced. I have no dependents. My dog does not have rabies. The septic tank has been recently drained. There is an unoccupied bedroom in my house. In the chest X-rays from my medical exam, there is no obstruction to the heart shown.

▲

There is a moving photo captioned, *Hazel Kempf, age 2*, in the newspaper printed the day after she was spared (and orphaned). She's in a hospital bed, sucking on cubes of sugar.

How long would readers have found her story sweet, would taxpayers have wanted to provide for her, though? How would she have fared today? Now, while our government fails to fund parental leave and child-care for workers, there's animus at *welfare mothers*.

People's treatment of others—and of other species of animals—reveals much about character. Consider how the men of Columbus treated the creatures who escaped from the train's wreckage. The monkeys and parrots were viewed as nuisances when no longer contained. Unlike the elephants and lions unified with their human keepers by burning, whom bystanders commented on mournfully, the species who slipped free were shot down from the trees and air.

At present, Americans opposed to reproductive rights seem more able to feel for the white spaces indicating embryos in ultrasounds than they do for born children, whose hearts actually beat as they struggle for years, long after they've learned to walk, through this world.

Hazel was raised by an aunt who is quoted by a reporter as saying, *She wasn't a beauty*. Still, when she was grown, Hazel, un-stymied, went to New York City to pursue show business.

Many mothers placing their infants for adoption are trying to raise children they already have, hold steady jobs, complete their educations, or reach other goals.

If a birth mother's life is insurmountably difficult and she doesn't achieve her dreams, at least her child will have better possibilities. That's cruelly compromised reassurance adoptive parents (actual or would-be like me) are forever trying to offer themselves.

I want to believe that what's most important in Hazel's story is that she became a performer, got the career she desired. As a character actor, her face continued to appear in print, in Camel cigarette and Tide detergent ads, wearing the expressions of the joker and the practical advisor. She stayed in the newspapers.

▲

Hazel married a magician. Maybe he could summon birds, maybe monkeys and other living creatures, from his top hat. Probably not. Maybe the magician conjured, like a trick with a mirror, through smoke, some allusion to what it might have been like if she'd been able to stay with her parents and the circus.

Many of the Hicks babies have searched for years to find their biological relations, had DNA tests, gone on national TV shows with their pleas for leads. Experiences like theirs are what led to the change to open adoption policies.

▲

The desire to know of one's origins is not a wish to do away with all the living that has happened since.

And if I bring my daughter to visit this graveyard, it need not be a macabre activity. We will walk among the bouquets, real and fake, and consider where we are not. She will not have been buried in the miniature lots of the Babyland section or I in the Strangers Grounds, for people, such as childless widows, whom no one cares to provide with a funeral.

▲

In ancient Roman culture, adoption was common. The motivations were money and power—to obtain a male inheritor or to build alliances between influential families. (And only boys were adopted.) But the positive interpretation I'm making of this fact is that the Romans—under whose rule culture advanced—were not hung up on bloodlines, as were the later medieval Europeans, characterized as regressive and inbred. Adopted children were a part of the legacy of what many argue is the civilization that most significantly shaped history.

If my daughter and I are walking in the graveyard, it will mean we are not buried anywhere yet. That we are living as people lucky to have a Saturday to spend observing, thinking of what we'll write or whatever record she'll make in the art form she prefers. That from within the boundaries of our bodies, we are at liberty to puzzle over others and the marks they leave.

▲

Columbus is home to the oldest survivor of the endangered stinking cedar (*Torreya taxifolia*) species. There used to be three of these trees in the city, but two died after a fire. Now the last one is dying out too, and scientists are taking cuttings to preserve the genetics. There doesn't seem to be any thought that the ancient tree itself can be saved. While reading about the stinking cedar, my eyes, browsing for optimistic news, stray to an article on the saplings the city is planting.

I am ready for when my daughter gets the common first grade assignment to draw a family tree. I have heard that many adoptive parents fear this exercise because of the questions it raises, but I am glad to do as counselors advise. I will label the trunk with the child's name, the roots with her birth mother's, and place her father's (my husband's) name and mine up in the branches with the leaves.

There's an initiative to add over nineteen thousand new trees to the streets, parks, and public spaces of Columbus because the city's canopy is *aging and declining,* says the news article. Included are plans for planting and landscaping—*greening*—this cemetery.

The adoptive version of the family tree may not make sense, biologically, but seems an improved representation in ways. A child will become the basis of my life when I become a mother, and the mother should fall before the child, and the tree should still stand after. Tree boughs without leaves in winter still have light shining between.

There were trees in the decorative cardboard Christmas village my grandmother passed down to me: twigs with bits of lichen spraypainted and pasted on. It's amazing, how those dry, delicate fibers, so long removed from the forest, have survived.

I won't necessarily know where my daughter gets sturdy knees from, if she has them, or whose hair and nose hers are like. Origins won't affect how I love the parts of the child I will see mature. They will be hers to stand on, grow out, and fill in.

But maybe my daughter's biological mother will want to keep in touch. I have come to hope that she does because I will be forever grateful to her for how our storylines intertwine, for being the genesis of the most important person who, for me, exists. Maybe she will send my daughter photos of her diploma or her new manicure or the view out her window when she moves, installments in a biography I'm fortunate to get to read as it is being written.

Why do I suppose anyone will be interested in reading the bits of information I have collected about history and adoption? Or interested in my experience with this uncommon method of building a family, which I haven't even completed yet? I just take pleasure in assembling my curious searches' results, capturing—or conveying—whatever words can. I hope relations between ideas can be discovered. Not comparisons between heartbreaks and ruptures but connections that people, working with more than heredity, forge.

After the wreck, the Model City was rebuilt. In a museum in Kempf's hometown, in this reincarnation, the railway is still in continuous operation, cars passing under its tiny yet proportionally grand trees. The stream Kempf designed to run down the little mountain could serve as a reminder of real nature, true rivers with water cycling back to refill them, part of a circle. Or a circle may be too tidy of a description. So, parts of an unclassifiable shape whose borders eventually wind around to join each other.

There are tunnels beneath the city of Columbus, and there have long been rumors that their purpose was to help enslaved people escape to safer states. More recently, under a historic mansion with lions flanking its doors, investigators found fish. These suggested a path that could be traced back to the Chattahoochee River and a different purpose for the tunnels. Even if they were not part of the Underground Railroad, the tunnels are still part of some mysterious marvel of a system.

▲

The fish were reminders that the city was constructed on former marshland. Where a six-story financial building now stands, there used to be a pond. White founders drained it and, scholars now suppose, built the tunnels to continue to siphon water away. Today, when the river rises, it stretches toward the site of the former pond, wanting to connect the parts of the watershed, erase banks' disunions.

And in the circus crash, the meeting of the trains was so emphatic, the two engines fused.

▲

My train trivia has collided with another story. Perhaps it seems that to arrive at some redemption, I am misconstruing legacies of obliteration. But the redemption will be in what is made real, by mothers and daughter, of themselves.

And I am right to see cemeteries as lovely; they're guaranteed green spaces even in the least prosperous cities. They do grow leaves out of decay. Walking away from the circus memorial, my mind keeps moving from the past fiery conclusion to the path over the earth ahead. This corner of Georgia is on the fall line between geological regions, where the stone and clay soil turns sandy. This place integrates the qualities of rivers with those of the sea.

▲

To counter ash and mud, I can say bedrock and flashes of creatures under water. To crash and flood, say intersections and branches. To blood and bound, answer: Daughter, wherever you come from, embark from here—

SOURCES

Thanks to the writers and editors of my references, including, but not limited to, the following, for the material I have quoted, collaged, braided, borrowed from, and used as beginnings for my explorations and imaginations.

"Weights and Measures": TheLiberalEquestrian.com provided a wealth of sources for this essay.

"Storied" is after and indebted to *Homeplace: The Social Use and Meaning of the Folk Dwelling in Southwestern North Carolina*, by Michael Ann Williams. It also quotes "An Interview with Lisa Lewis," by Jeff Simpson, in *The Fiddleback*; "The 'I' of Lyric," by Dan Beachy-Quick, in the *Boston Review*; and the books *The Little Death of the Self*, by Marianne Boruch, and *Streaming*, by Allison Adelle Hedge Coke.

"Circling" draws much of its information from *Monuments to the Lost Cause*, edited by Cynthia Mills and Pamela H. Simpson, particularly from the chapters "Gratitude and Gender Wars," by Mills, and "Commemorating the Color Line," by Micki McElya. The historical information about Macon County, North Carolina comes from WomensHistoryTrail.org, unpublished papers from Barbara McRae, and conversations with Mary Polanski.

"Service" quotes the *Rubaiyat of Omar Khayyam* as translated by Peter Avery and John Heath-Stubbs and was sparked by the *Guardian*'s article by Jenny Uglow, "The Great Crash."

"A Lily Is a Lily Is a Lily" is influenced by many gardening catalogs and websites. John B. Silk's "The Adaptive Value of Sociality in Mammalian Groups" was central to my reading about primates.

"Your Lot" adapts quotations in exhibits at the Chipley Historical Center in Pine Mountain, Georgia, and Troup County Archives and Legacy Museum in LaGrange, Georgia.

"Between States" quotes "They Know Too Much Already: Black Education in Post-Emancipation Era Columbus, GA, 1866–1876," by William Dwayne Thomas.

"Fragmental; or, Rocks Prone to Fragmentation Create Soils That Are Going to Erode": *Let Us Now Praise Famous Gullies: Providence Canyon and the Soils of the South,* by Paul S. Sutter, provided not only facts but broader ways of thinking about Providence Canyon and the southern landscape. I also referred to "The Father of Soil Conservation," an article on PBS.org, and GeorgiaEncyclopedia.org as I wrote this essay.

The orphanage records adapted for use in "(Un) Disclosed" can be found in Columbus State University Archives and Special Collections, Columbus, GA.

"A Door Is a Threshold in Which You Can Turn Either Way" began with reading *The Antique Doorknob,* by Maud L. Eastwood.

WABE.org, the website of Atlanta's NPR and PBS affiliate, educated me about the Flint River as I drafted "A Good Pour."

"Several Smaller Stones" is built with quotations from *Practical Stone Masonry Made Easy,* by Stephen M. Kennedy

Quotes in "Negative" come from "Jubilat Agno," by Christopher Smart; *Faithful and Virtuous Night,* by Louise Glück; *Platero and I,* by Juan Ramón Jiménez; and *Why Look at Animals?,* by John Berger.

"Another Inscrutable House": This essay quotes Ben Lerner's "Postscript: C. D. Wright" in the *New Yorker* and Mark Nowak's review, *Deepstep Come Shining*, in *Rain Taxi*, and is informed by other writings such as "Lyric Essentials: Bradley Trumpfheller Reads C. D. Wright" from Sundress Publications. The poems by C. D. Wright I reference are "hills: an autobiographical preface," from *Further Adventures with You*; "The Next to the Last Draft," from *Steal Away*; and *Deepstep Come Shining*. The essay also quotes Jericho Brown's piece "Invention," from the Poetry Foundation website, Poetry.com; Ellen Bryant Voigt's "Noble Dog," from *Headwaters*, and "Who said the worst was past, who knew," from *Kyrie*; Elizabeth Bishop's "Jeronimo's House," from *North & South*, and "Sestina," from *Questions of Travel*; *Let Us Now Praise Famous Men*, by James Agee and Walker Evans; *Houses without Names: Architectural Nomenclature and the Classification of America's Common Houses*, by Thomas C. Hubka; and *Vernacular Architecture*, by Henry Glassie.

"Settling In" quotes "It All Happened in Pine Mountain Valley," by Paul K. Conkin, in the *Georgia Historical Quarterly*; Civilian Conservation Corps and Forest Service, "Acceptable Building Plans"; and the poetry collection *Light Wind Light Light*, by Bin Ramke. Details in this essay have been changed so that characters and places resemble but should not be identified as actual people and exact locations.

When writing "Without Conclusion," though I have failed to learn any Tsalagi, I explored the Cherokee language learning program at YourGrandMothersCherokee.com and the site Native-Languages.org. I read many articles in the *Cherokee One Feather* and other western North Carolina newspapers, relying especially on "Cracking the code to speak Cherokee," by Dale Neal, in the *Asheville Citizen-Times*, and learned from the *Appalachian Voices*' piece by Elizabeth E. Payne, "New Program Makes Learning Cherokee Easier."

"Railway Coupling" derives information about the train crash and Riverdale Cemetery from AtlasObscura.com; RoadsideAmerica.com; "Circus Wreck: 100 Years Ago, a Fiery Rail Crash Destroyed a Circus and Gave

Columbus a Tiny Hero," by Richard Hyatt, published in the *Columbus Ledger-Enquirer*; and *Jamestown Weekly Alert*, a North Dakota newspaper. I gleaned information about Kempf's model city from UpNorthMichigan.com and *Popular Electricity and the World's Advocate* (1911). Information on the Hicks babies comes from a series in the *Atlanta Journal-Constitution*. Information on stinking cedars is thanks to TorreyaGuardians.com and information on the tunnels is thanks to "What Folklore Erases: Under Columbus, Georgia," by Bryan Banks, in PublicBooks.org.

ACKNOWLEDGMENTS

I must thank Anna V. Q. Ross for her essential role in my completing this book and Justin Gardiner for everything—particularly for bringing so many exemplary essays into our house. I am grateful to my readers Jessica Jacobs, Rachel Howard, Lia Greenwell, Austin Segrest, and MRB Chelko. (It seems I'm going to have to thank some of you in all the books I write.) I appreciate the support of my colleagues at Auburn University as well as of my students. And most of all, I am indebted to the family members who are the starting point and substance of any story I might call mine.

The essays in this book appeared in the following journals, sometimes in different forms and with different titles. My thanks to the editors whose suggestions made my writing better.

"A Door Is a Threshold in Which You Can Turn Either Way" and "Service," *Seneca Review* 51, no. 2 (Fall 2021).

"A Good Pour," "No Dummy," and "Several Smaller Stones," *Ninth Letter* 21, no. 3 (Spring–Summer 2025).

"A Lily Is a Lily Is a Lily," *Zone 3* 9, no. 1 (April 2024).

"Another Inscrutable House," *Annulet Poetics Journal* 1 (April 2021).

"Between States," *The Common*, September 14, 2022.

"Blueprints," *Blackbird* 18, no. 2 (Fall 2019).

"Circling," *North American Review* (Fall 2025).

"Fragmental; or, Rocks Prone to Fragmentation Create Soils That Are Going to Erode," *CutBank Literary Magazine* 98, no. 1 (Spring 2023).

"Instructions for Conducting a Cemetery Survey," "Mountain Music," and "Reintroduction," *Appalachian Voices*, November 26, 2024.

"Negative," *Bluestem* (Summer–Fall 2023).

"Remains to See," *Orion* (June 2020).

"Storied," *Ecotone* 18.2, no. 34 (Summer 2023).

"Vessels," *Global South* 16, no. 1 (Summer 2023).

"Weights and Measures," *Shenandoah* 68, no. 1 (Fall 2018).

"Without Conclusion," *Florida Review* 48, no. 2 (Spring 2025).

Finally, a deep thank you to James W. Long, Ashley Gilly, and the staff at LSU Press.

www.ingramcontent.com/pod-product-compliance
Lightning Source LLC
Chambersburg PA
CBHW020021030726
47499CB00007B/2213